REVISE EDEXCEL GCSE
History A
The Making of the Modern World
For the linear specification first teaching 2013

REVISION GUIDE

Series Consultant: Harry Smith

Author: Rob Bircher

A note from the publisher

In order to ensure that this resource offers high-quality support for the associated Pearson qualification, it has been through a review process by the awarding body. This process confirms that this resource fully covers the teaching and learning content of the specification or part of a specification at which it is aimed. It also confirms that it demonstrates an appropriate balance between the development of subject skills, knowledge and understanding, in addition to preparation for assessment.

Endorsement does not cover any guidance on assessment activities or processes (e.g. practice questions or advice on how to answer assessment questions), included in the resource nor does it prescribe any particular approach to the teaching or delivery of a related course.

While the publishers have made every attempt to ensure that advice on the qualification and its assessment is accurate, the official specification and associated assessment guidance materials are the only authoritative source of information and should always be referred to for definitive guidance.

Pearson examiners have not contributed to any sections in this resource relevant to examination papers for which they have responsibility.

Examiners will not use endorsed resources as a source of material for any assessment set by Pearson.

Endorsement of a resource does not mean that the resource is required to achieve this Pearson qualification, nor does it mean that it is the only suitable material available to support the qualification, and any resource lists produced by the awarding body shall include this and other appropriate resources.

For the full range of Pearson revision titles across GCSE, AS/A Level and BTEC visit:
www.pearsonschools.co.uk/revise

ALWAYS LEARNING

PEARSON

Contents

> ✓ Make sure you know which topics you've studied – you only need to revise these!

A small bit of small print

Pearson publishes Sample Assessment Material and the Specification on its website. This is the official content and this book should be used in conjunction with it. The questions in *Now try this* have been written to help you practise every topic in the book. Remember: the real exam questions may not look like this.

How did the Cold War begin?

As the Second World War ended, the Grand Alliance of the USA, USSR and Britain made agreements at three conferences about what would happen to Europe. Tensions between the Allies grew into the Cold War.

Teheran Conference (1943)

Stalin wanted the Allies to attack Germany in Europe to take pressure off the USSR. Churchill wanted this attack to be in the Balkans, but Stalin objected: the USSR should have influence in Eastern Europe, and the USA and Britain in Western Europe.

Yalta Conference (1945)

It was agreed that the USSR would help defeat Japan, that all Allies would work for democracy in Europe and that the UN would be set up to promote peace.

Potsdam Conference (1945)

Decisions were made on what to do with Germany: prosecute Nazis as war criminals, reduce the size of Germany by a quarter and divide Germany up temporarily into French, British, US and Soviet quarters. Reparations to be taken from each zone.

Tensions within the Grand Alliance

Europe should be democratic – a capitalist democracy. Roosevelt believed that democracy meant different political parties working to win voters' support in free elections.

What should happen to Germany? Germany should have to pay reparations, ensuring that it is never strong enough to start another war.

What should happen to Germany? Germany should be rebuilt.

Europe should be democratic – a communist democracy. Stalin believed that because only communism truly represented the workers, democracies could only be communist.

The USA was the first to build an atomic bomb, which gave it an unbeatable advantage (until 1949, when the USSR caught up).

The USSR didn't do what it said it would do in Poland: the government was supposed to include multiple political parties, but actually was only a communist democracy.

Now try this

1   What were the main decisions of the Teheran, Yalta and Potsdam conferences?

2   The USSR said communism could be democratic too: what was the Western criticism of communist democracy?

EXAM ALERT!

Students often confuse Teheran, Yalta and Potsdam. Make sure you are clear about what decisions were made at each conference.

Students have struggled with this topic in recent exams – **be prepared!**

Results Plus

Breakdown of trust

Without a common enemy to fight, tensions between the USA and USSR intensified. Neither side trusted the other.

Ideology

Understanding ideology – a set of political ideas about how society should be run – is key to understanding the Cold War. The USA and the USSR had opposing ideologies.

The USA

Said communism enslaved people to the state. Capitalism was based on freedom and democracy:

- Everyone should be free to make money for themselves.

- Individuals are better at deciding what to make/sell than the state.

- Trade between countries makes everyone richer.

The USSR

Said capitalism exploited the workers to make the rich even richer. Communism was based on fairness:

- Capitalism only makes some people rich by exploiting everyone else.

- Individuals are not as strong as everyone working together for the same aim.

- The state should take control of the economy and run it to benefit everyone.

The Long Telegram (1946)

A secret report from the US ambassador Kennan in Moscow to President Truman said:

- the USSR saw capitalism as a threat to communism that had to be destroyed

- the USSR was building its military power

- peace between a communist USSR and a capitalist USA was not possible.

Novikov's Telegram (1946)

A report from Novikov, Soviet ambassador to the USA, told Stalin that:

- the USA wanted world domination and was building up its military strength

- the USSR was the only country left after the war that could stand up to the USA

- the USA was preparing its people for war with the USSR.

Timeline

Nuclear arms race

1945 USA drops two atomic bombs on Japanese cities

1949 USSR tests its first atomic bomb

1952 USA develops H-bomb (hydrogen bomb)

1953 USSR develops H-bomb

Both superpowers having nuclear weapons was a powerful reason why a cold war did not become a hot war!

Now try this

1   Create a table with two columns, one for capitalism and the other for communism. Then, insert any words that relate to either, matching words by their opposing term (e.g. capitalism: individual / communism: collective).

2   Now answer the following questions in the light of the table you have just created:
    (a) What was communism's main criticism of capitalism?
    (b) What was capitalism's main criticism of communism?

Creating lists like these will help you associate with the terms and topic, plus draw conclusions about the main criticisms/issues. You can use this method for any topic really!

Satellite states, Cominform and Comecon

Between 1947 and 1949, the USSR spread its sphere of influence to neighbouring countries. Countries like Poland and Hungary became 'satellite states' under the control of the USSR.

Communism and 'free' elections

- At the Yalta and Potsdam conferences, the USSR agreed to free elections in the countries in its sphere of influence.
- The USSR thought people would choose communism in free elections however, most did not.
- So the USSR fixed elections making sure the Communist Party won.
- Once in power, the communists shut down the opposition parties and each country became a single-party state.

Legend:
- Land taken by USSR at the end of Second World War
- Soviet-controlled communist countries
- Non Soviet-controlled communist countries

Map labels: ESTONIA, LATVIA, LITHUANIA, BALTIC STATES, Berlin, EAST GERMANY, POLAND, USSR, CZECH, AUSTRIA, HUNGARY, ROMANIA, YUGOSLAVIA, BULGARIA, ALBANIA. 400 km

Soviet expansion in Europe, 1945–48.

Cominform

Cominform stood for the Communist Information Bureau. Stalin set it up in 1947. The bureau organised all the communist parties in Europe and arranged their leadership so they would do what Moscow told them to.

Key points:

- Cominform got rid of any opposition to the USSR's control in satellite states.
- It encouraged communist parties in Western countries to block Marshall Plan assistance.

Comecon

Comecon stood for the Council for Mutual Economic Assistance. Stalin set it up in 1949. It was the USSR's alternative to the Marshall Plan.

Key points:

- It built up trade links between Comecon countries.
- It also prevented Comecon countries signing up to the Marshall Plan.
- Comecon included the USSR, Bulgaria, Czechoslovakia, Hungary, Poland, Romania, Albania and, from 1950, the German Democratic Republic (East Germany).

Consequences

Western Europe was now in one camp. It was linked to the USA through the Marshall Plan and the US policy of containment of communism.

⟷

Eastern Europe was now in one camp. It was tied to the USSR as satellite states and the USSR believed socialist revolution would spread worldwide.

Now try this

1. Briefly describe Cominform and Comecon's key points.
2. Why was Stalin so keen to prevent satellite countries getting money from the Marshall Plan?

The Truman Doctrine and the Marshall Plan

In response to the spread of Soviet control in Eastern Europe, the USA stepped up its involvement in Europe, and the USSR was determined to defend itself against ideological attack from the West. The USA was determined to stop the spread of communism, and the USSR was determined to defend itself against Western attack. Europe was the centre of this ideological 'battleground'.

Truman's concerns

- Europe was devastated after the war.
- In many countries people had no money, no jobs and were feeling hopeless.
- Communism was attractive to people: it made sure everyone had enough.
- Many in Eastern Europe had been liberated from Nazi rule by the Soviets.
- Countries like Poland, Romania and Bulgaria had already had communist governments forced on them.
- Some governments (e.g. Greece and Turkey) were too poor to combat communist revolutions in their own countries.
- If Greece and Turkey became communist, then other countries across Europe and the Middle East would follow.

Post-war Berlin

The Truman Doctrine (1947)

In a speech in 1947, US President Truman set out why the USA should get involved:
- Countries faced a choice between either capitalism or communism.
- Communism was bad because it meant people could not be free.
- The USA must try to contain (hold back) this spread of communism.
- The USA should provide money and troops (if necessary) to help free governments to combat communist takeovers.

The Marshall Plan (1947)

- $13 billion from USA to help rebuild Europe.
- Communism appealed most to people with nothing to lose, so the Marshall Plan hoped to stop communism by giving people a stake in the capitalist system.
- Countries must trade with the USA to get the money.
- Sixteen Western European countries took the money.
- The USSR criticised the Marshall Plan as an attack on them.

Now try this

1 Explain **three** reasons why President Truman was worried about communism spreading in Europe.

2 Explain why the USA hoped that the Marshall Plan would combat the spread of communism.

The Berlin Blockade

The Allies were unable to agree about Germany's post-war future. A short-term solution was to divide the country and its capital, Berlin. The USSR felt threatened by the USA's rebuilding of western Germany.

Reunification

The USA wanted a united, capitalist Germany that it could trade with and would help prevent the spread of communism.

Division

The USSR wanted Germany to be weak, communist and divided, so that it would never be able to attack the USSR again.

Bizonia and western Germany

- It made sense for British and US zones to join together, as it would be easier to administer. The area was called Bizonia and was included in the Marshall Plan.
- This was *not* popular with the USSR, as Stalin was not consulted. He thought Bizonia went against the agreements made at the Potsdam Conference, and he suspected the USA was aiming to permanently divide richer western Germany from poorer eastern Germany.

Eastern Germany and the Berlin Blockade

- The USSR had 1.5 million troops in its zone, whereas the Western countries had sent most of their troops home.
- Eastern Germany grew almost all the food that western Germany ate.
- Berlin was deep in USSR-controlled Germany, and divided into US, British, French and Soviet zones.
- The USSR blocked all supplies into Berlin to show it had the power to stop a divided Germany working.

The Berlin airlift

West Berlin couldn't last for many days without supplies. It looked like the Western powers would have to pull out of Berlin. That would look weak, undermining the USA's image in particular. So Western powers responded with an airlift – thousands of tonnes of supplies were flown into Berlin.

West Germany

- The Berlin airlift made the USA appear peaceful and generous.
- In September 1949, West Germany (FRG) was officially formed, with US support.
- In 1949, Western European countries and the USA formed NATO to counter the Soviet military threat.

East Germany

- The Berlin Blockade made the USSR appear aggressive and threatening.
- In October 1949, East Germany (GDR) was officially formed as a Soviet state.
- In 1955, the USSR formed the Warsaw Pact to counter the military threat from NATO.

Now try this

1 What were the FRG, GDR and NATO?
2 If the Soviets had 1.5 million troops in Germany and the USA only had a few hundred thousand, suggest **one** reason why the USSR didn't just invade western Germany and take over.

Soviet control in Hungary

After Stalin died, Soviet leader Khrushchev indicated Soviet control would relax. But when Hungary started to move away from Soviet influence, the USSR tightened its control for fear that if Hungary left the Warsaw Pact, other countries would follow.

Impact of Soviet rule

👎 Hungary suffered a lot under Stalin's control.

👎 Food and industrial products were shipped off to Russia.

👎 Any opposition in Hungary was ruthlessly wiped out.

👎 Matyas Rakosi was a brutal ruler.

👎 Communist rule became very unpopular.

De-Stalinisation

When Stalin died, Khrushchev took over. In 1956 Khrushchev hinted that control would relax. Hungarians started demonstrating against communist control. Khrushchev appointed a more liberal leader for Hungary: Imre Nagy.

The Hungarian uprising in 1956, showing a statue of Stalin that had been pulled down.

Imre Nagy wanted **reforms** for Hungary which were as follows:

✓ leave the Warsaw Pact

✓ no more communist government

✓ free elections, democracy

✓ UN protection from USSR.

Khrushchev refused Nagy's demands – if Hungary left the Warsaw Pact, other countries would soon follow.

✗ November 1956: Khrushchev sent 200 000 Soviet troops into Hungary.

✗ Thousands were killed as a result.

✗ Imre Nagy was tried and executed.

International reaction and consequences

The United Nations condemned Soviet actions. Some countries boycotted the 1956 Olympics in protest. But stronger actions did not happen.	The USA supported Hungary's uprising – with money, medical aid and words. The USA accepted 80 000 refugees from Hungary.	But the USA couldn't send troops: would risk nuclear war.	Hungary was on its own against the USSR: they had to give in.	Satellite states saw that the USA would not defend them against the USSR. Soviet control retightened across Eastern Europe.

Now try this

Draw up a timeline showing the key events in how the Cold War developed, 1943–56.

A divided Berlin

After the war, Germany was divided into four zones and its capital city, Berlin, was also divided into four. The divided city became a focus for the Cold War.

- Berlin was deep inside Soviet-controlled East Germany.

- Divided Berlin gave the USA a foothold inside the Soviet **Eastern Bloc**.

- Some Germans in East Germany did not like having a communist government.

- There were also better jobs with higher wages in the West.

- It was easy to get to West Germany once you had reached the western zones in Berlin.

- Many Germans crossed over from the East to the West in Berlin.

- Many skilled workers left for the West, leaving the East with a skills shortage.

- This looked very bad for the Soviets: people clearly preferred West Germany to East Germany.

The division of Germany after 1945.

Khrushchev's ultimatum (November 1958) announced that all Berlin belonged to East Germany: all occupying troops must leave in six months.

The USSR knew that if it tried to push the West out of Berlin by force, a war would start that it could not win...

Reasons for attacking West Berlin	Reasons for not attacking West Berlin
✓ There are many more Soviet troops than Western troops around Berlin and in Germany...	✗ ... but the USA has developed the H-bomb (1952).
✓ So the Soviet army could easily defeat a Western allied army...	✗ ... but the USA has 20 times more H-bombs than the USSR.
✓ The USSR has also developed an H-bomb (1953)...	✗ ... but the USA has money to develop and build B52 bombers, which can fly 6000 miles.
This means that the USA could drop H-bombs on the USSR but the USSR couldn't drop them on the USA.	

Now try this

1. The Eastern Bloc was made up of the Warsaw Pact countries. But what was the Warsaw Pact?

2. Why was West Berlin a problem for the USSR?

7

The Berlin Wall

The USSR and USA started negotiations to sort out the Berlin problem, but they broke down. Khrushchev's solution was the Berlin Wall.

The USSR demanded withdrawal

The Soviets could not continue to allow Germans to leave East Germany through Berlin. So they announced (November 1958) that Berlin was East German and that the Western powers must leave the city in six months – or else.

The USA objected

The USA did not want to leave Berlin as it would be humiliating. But it didn't want to start a war, either. Instead, the USA suggested a conference to sort the problems out.

The USSR and the USA met **four times** (at big conferences called summits):

1 May 1959 – in Geneva

2 September 1959 – US President Eisenhower met Khrushchev (Camp David, USA)

3 May 1960 – second Eisenhower-Khrushchev meeting (Paris)

4 June 1961 – meeting between Khrushchev and the new US president, J.F. Kennedy (Vienna).

What happened at the summits?

The first two summits went fairly well, though no solution was agreed. However, the third summit was a disaster – a US spy plane had been shot down over the USSR and Eisenhower refused to apologise and the summit collapsed. The final summit was only agreed because there was a new US president but neither side was willing to back down. Kennedy began to prepare the USA for nuclear war.

1 Khrushchev backed down: as he knew he couldn't win a nuclear war.

2 Western powers stayed in Berlin.

3 Instead, the Berlin Wall was built (from August 1961).

4 Anyone trying to escape was shot at. Many people were killed.

5 The wall stopped East Germans leaving for the West, which solved the crisis.

6 This way, Khrushchev avoided war with USA but still looked strong.

Remember that JFK's visit to West Berlin in 1963 had a huge impact. His speech made West Berlin into a symbol of freedom.

Now try this

1 Explain what the six-month ultimatum was.

2 Was the Berlin Wall:

   A ☐ built across Berlin

   B ☐ built around Germany

   C ☐ built around the whole Eastern Bloc?

EXAM ALERT!

Do not confuse the Berlin Blockade with the Berlin Wall.

Students have struggled with this topic in recent exams – **be prepared!**

ResultsPlus

The Cuban Missile Crisis: origins

A revolution in Cuba set it against its neighbour, the USA. The USA attempted to bring Cuba back into its sphere of influence but, instead, Cuba asked the USSR for help with defence.

Cuba, the USA and the USSR

Before 1959, Cuba was very closely linked to the USA, for example, there were lots of US-owned businesses. Then Cuba had a socialist revolution in 1959 and the USA refused to deal with the new government. So, instead, Cuba started to build **economic links** with the USSR, trading for example, Soviet oil for Cuban sugar. The US relationship with Cuba deteriorated.

Get Castro!

Fidel Castro

- The USA did not want a socialist country in their sphere of influence.
- Especially not a country with close links to the USSR.
- The CIA tried to assassinate the leader of Cuba Fidel Castro with no success.
- The CIA convinced President Kennedy that a US-backed invasion of Cuba could solve the problem.

The Bay of Pigs incident – 17 April 1961

What the CIA told Kennedy

- ✓ The invasion will look like a Cuban revolt – we've trained Cuban exiles and disguised old US planes as Cuban.
- ✓ Castro's control of Cuba is very weak.
- ✓ Most Cubans hate Castro.

What actually happened

- ✗ The planes were recognised as US planes and photographed, and the information was published. The world knew that the USA had backed the invasion.
- ✗ In fact, Castro knew of the invasion in advance and 1400 US-backed troops met 20 000 of Castro's troops. The US-backed troops surrendered.
- ✗ In fact, most Cubans did not want their old leader, Batista, back again, because he had been corrupt.

The impact

- Ended all chance of a friendly USA-Cuba relationship.
- Castro announced that he was a communist.
- Cuba and the USSR started building closer ties – including military defence for Cuba...

Now try this

Describe the Bay of Pigs incident in your own words. What did President Kennedy think would happen and why did it fail?

The Cuban Missile Crisis: the discovery

When the USA discovered the USSR's missile sites on Cuba, the USA was torn on how best to respond: attack while it could or do everything possible to avoid war.

The Cuban missile sites

MEDIUM RANGE BALLISTIC MISSILE BASE IN CUBA
SAN CRISTOBAL

The USSR saw Cuba as a fix to a key strategic problem: the USA had missiles close to the USSR (e.g. in the UK), but the USSR had no missiles close to the USA.

Cuba saw Soviet missiles as a great way to prevent the USA from invading Cuba again.

In September 1962, Soviet ships carried nuclear warheads and missiles to Cuba.

Then in October 1962, US spy planes photographed the Cuban missile sites and the secret was out.

The US public learned that they were now in range of Soviet nuclear missiles. There was panic.

How should the USA respond?

President Kennedy and his team thought through the different options. Some advisors (the '**hawks**') wanted to attack straight away, while others (the '**doves**') wanted to avoid nuclear war if at all possible.

Ignore the Cuban missiles: the USA also had many missile bases close to the USSR, for example, in Turkey.

Do a deal and get the USSR to withdraw from Cuba in return for the USA withdrawing from one of its missile bases close to the USSR.

Invade Cuba: US troops would invade and get rid of the Castro government.

Nuclear attack: attack the USSR quickly before the USSR could attack the USA.

Warn Castro that his actions put Cuba in grave danger and hope that Castro would decide to stop the missile site construction.

Blockade Cuba to stop any more missiles or equipment coming from the USSR.

Destroy Cuban missile sites. This could be done with airstrikes and so wouldn't need nuclear strikes or a land invasion.

Now try this

If you were an advisor to President Kennedy, which option would you have recommended and why?

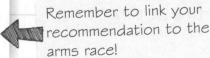
Remember to link your recommendation to the arms race!

The Cuban Missile Crisis: the Thirteen Days

The Thirteen Days was a period during the Cuban Missile Crisis when the world came very close to nuclear war.

Timeline

1962

16 Oct President Kennedy is informed that US spy planes have found missile sites on Cuba

20 Oct Kennedy decides against an attack. Orders a blockade of Cuba

24 Oct USSR says a blockade is an act of aggression and its ships will ignore it

25 Oct USA and USSR prepare for immediate nuclear attack

27 Oct Cuba gets ready for invasion

Khrushchev offers to remove missiles from Cuba if USA does the same from its Italy and Turkey bases

A US spy plane is shot down over Cuba. US hawks demand retaliation

Robert Kennedy sets up a deal in which the USA would secretly withdraw warheads from Italy and Turkey

28 Oct Khrushchev agrees to the deal: missiles withdrawn in return for USA agreeing never to attack Cuba and taking its missiles out of Italy and Turkey

Short-term consequences

- Cuba came out OK, but was let down by Soviet allies.
- The USSR looked weak as no one knew about the USA's withdrawals.
- US 'doves' came out well as US 'hawks' would have gone to war.

Long-term consequences

The Cuban Missile Crisis showed how easily a nuclear war could start. The USA initiated a move to **détente** – a less stressful, more informed relationship between the USA and the USSR.

- The **Hotline Agreement** created a direct communication link between Washington and Moscow.
- **Limited Test Ban Treaty** (August 1963) – both sides agreed to ban all nuclear weapon testing except for underground tests.
- In 1963 Kennedy gave a speech about working with the USSR to focus on their 'common interests'.
- However, the USSR was determined to catch up with USA in the arms race and achieved this by 1965. This meant **Mutually Assured Destruction** (MAD). War would be so terrible that it must be avoided at all costs.
- Khrushchev was forced from power in 1964.

Now try this

1. If the USA had missile bases close to the USSR, why did the USA object so much to the USSR having bases close to it? Explain your reasons.

2. Explain how far MAD contributed to peace.

EXAM ALERT!

Make sure you are clear about the chronology of the Cuban Missile Crisis.

Students have struggled with this topic in recent exams – **be prepared!**

 ResultsPlus

Soviet control in Czechoslovakia

Like in Hungary, a relaxation of control in a satellite state led to a challenge to Soviet authority. When the USSR used force to get back control, splits appeared in the Eastern Bloc.

The impact of Soviet rule on Czechoslovakia

- Czechoslovakia's economy and living standards declined.
- Any opposition to communism was crushed.
- Communist rule became very unpopular.

Brezhnev and Dubček

Alexander Dubček

- In January 1968 Dubček became the Czechoslovakian leader.
- He was a good friend of Soviet leader Leonid Brezhnev.
- He was a communist and supporter of the Warsaw Pact but wanted to make communism better and easier to live under.
- His reforms resulted in the 'Prague Spring' – a period of increased political freedom – in April 1968 and lots of criticism of communism resulted.

Dubček's reforms

Relaxation of censorship meant more freedom to say and write things, even if critical of communism. More democracy allowed other parties alongside the Communist Party. More power was given to the Czech parliament and Soviet control was reduced.

Brezhnev's response

Brezhnev could not allow the reforms, as any weakness in control could mean the break-up of the Warsaw Pact – even though this wasn't Dubček's intention. Brezhnev failed to convince Dubček to stop the reforms. In August 1968, the USSR sent tanks to Prague and Dubček was arrested. Czechoslovakia returned to being under strict Soviet control.

Consequences

The Brezhnev Doctrine – from now on, the USSR declared the right to invade any Eastern Bloc country that was threatening the security of the Eastern Bloc as a whole.	The USA condemned the invasion but did nothing to stop it: it feared war.	Western European communist parties were horrified and declared themselves independent from the Soviet Communist Party.	Yugoslavia and Romania also backed off from the USSR, weakening the USSR's grip on Eastern Europe.

Now try this

Draw up a timeline showing the key events in the Cold War 1957–68.

Remember to think about the different places where events took place and the actions of the USA and USSR

Détente

Détente is a French word meaning the relaxing of tension between rivals. It was used to describe the relationship between the USA and the USSR in the later 1960s and 1970s. Here are some key examples of détente in practice:

Outer Space Treaty (1967)

- No nuclear weapons in space.

Nuclear Non-Proliferation Treaty (1968)

An agreement to prevent the spread of nuclear weapons. (USA, USSR, UK, France and China had nuclear weapons.)

- Countries with nuclear weapons would not help other countries get them too.
- Countries without nuclear weapons would not try to get them.
- Countries with nuclear weapons agreed to talk about disarmament.

SALT 1 – Strategic Arms Limitation Treaty (1972)

Superpowers agreed to limit the number of nuclear weapons they had.

- No further production of strategic ballistic weapons (short-range, lightweight missiles).
- No increase in number of intercontinental ballistic weapons (though new ones could be added to replace old ones).
- No new nuclear missile launchers. New submarines that could launch nuclear weapons only allowed as replacements for existing missile launchers.
- The Anti-Ballistic Missile (ABM) Treaty limited both sides to two ABM deployment areas.

1975 Helsinki Conference

Representatives from 35 countries, including the USSR and the USA, agreed on security issues, co-operation, human rights and borders.

Agreement on borders: East and West Germany accepted each other officially

Trade co-operation: the USA agreed to buy oil from the USSR and the USSR agreed to buy wheat from the USA

All disputes to be settled peacefully, through the UN if necessary

Sharing of scientific knowledge (e.g. in medicine) and educational co-operation (e.g. student exchanges)

No country to interfere in the internal affairs of another country

Countries to respect human rights, including freedom of speech, religion, movement and information

Now try this

1. Write your own definition of détente.
2. Explain why the superpowers were interested in nuclear non-proliferation.

It's important to remember there were limitations to détente. The superpowers still had thousands of nuclear weapons targeted on each other, and they were still competing to gain influence in countries. Also, the USSR didn't honour the human rights agreements from the Helsinki Accords.

The Soviet invasion of Afghanistan

Brezhnev gambled that the USA wouldn't do anything if the USSR clamped down on trouble in Afghanistan. But the US reaction revived the Cold War and put an end to détente.

The Soviet invasion

In 1968 the USSR sent tanks into Czechoslovakia to put down anti-communist groups. The USA condemned this, but didn't do anything.

In 1979, the USSR sent troops into Afghanistan, a country with a communist government, to take control after the president was assassinated. This time the USA reacted very strongly.

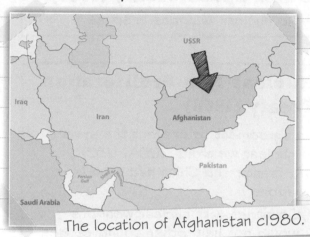

The location of Afghanistan c1980.

The Carter Doctrine – January 1980

US President Jimmy Carter took the following actions:

- He threatened to use force if the USSR attempted to take control of the Persian Gulf.
- Economic sanctions – no trade with the USSR.
- Set up an alliance with China and Israel to back Afghan rebels (Mujahideen) against the Soviets.
- The USA secretly provided weapons and money to the Mujahideen.
- The USA broke off diplomatic relations with the USSR and refused to sign SALT 2.
- The USA boycotted 1980 Olympic Games in Moscow, which led to the USSR boycotting 1984 Olympic Games in Los Angeles.

SALT 2

- In negotiation since 1972.
- Planned to reduce stocks to 2250 warheads per superpower.
- Imposed limits on new launch systems.

Why did Carter react so strongly?

The USA was worried that the USSR would get more control in the Middle East. Afghanistan might mean Soviet influence in Iran.

Iran could block Middle East oil exports at the Straits of Hormuz. Middle East oil was essential to the USA's prosperity.

Afghanistan and the superpowers

Before the war, the USSR had backed the socialist Afghan government. But the USA was secretly funding the Afghan opposition to the government. So when the rebels started to fight the government, the government asked the USSR for help.

Now try this

1 Explain what reaction the USSR expected from the USA in December 1979.

2 Give reasons for the USA's response to the Soviet invasion of Afghanistan.

The Second Cold War, 1979-85

Ronald Reagan became US president in 1981. He believed that the USA had a mission from God to win the Cold War.

Mutually Assured Destruction (MAD)

Previously, nuclear strategy was based on MAD. As long as the USA and USSR would both destroy each other (and everyone else) in a nuclear war, it was too risky for either side to start one.

A nuclear explosion

Strategic Defense Initiative (SDI)

But President Reagan wanted to win the Cold War, so he launched SDI, known as 'Star Wars'. SDI was a plan to have satellites in space that would destroy Soviet intercontinental nuclear missiles before they reached the USA.

Star Wars

Reagan and the 'Evil Empire'

President Reagan made no efforts to get détente up and running again.

* In fact, he described the USSR as an 'Evil Empire' – this was not diplomatic!
* As well as SDI, which was never built as planned, he kick-started the arms race again.
* US technology was developing fast in the 1980s, especially computing.
* The USA poured money into developing new missile technology.

Crisis in the USSR

The USSR could not keep up with the USA.

* Its economy was in poor shape, partly because it spent so much on weapons.
* Living standards were very low right across the Eastern Bloc.
* It was bogged down in the war in Afghanistan.
* The USSR did not have the USA's computing expertise.
* The USSR had given everything to keep up with the USA, but SDI pushed the arms race beyond it.

Now try this

Explain how SDI changed the relationship between the USA and the USSR.

Gorbachev's new thinking

In 1985, Mikhail Gorbachev became leader of the USSR – he was to be its last leader. Gorbachev tried to reform the Soviet Union in order to solve its economic, social and political stagnation. He rejected any argument that this meant capitalism had won: he felt he was making socialism stronger.

Gorbachev as leader

Recognised that the economy was failing.

Recognised that the Soviet people were unhappy and distrustful of government.

Brought in *perestroika* (restructuring). It meant new ways of doing things.

Brought in *glasnost* (openness). It meant more freedom for people to say what they really thought.

Foreign relations changed – more open and positive.

Desperate to get the USSR out of the war in Afghanistan.

Mikhail Gorbachev

Was very slow to allow democratic elections in USSR.

Tried to cover up the scale of the massive nuclear accident at Chernobyl.

Did not want capitalism, just a stronger socialism.

Never planned to cause end of USSR.

Geneva, November 1985

- Gorbachev and Reagan met at the Geneva summit.

- The two men got on well and agreed to more meetings.

Reykjavik, October 1986

- Reagan and Gorbachev said they would work to cut down the number of nuclear weapons they had.

- Gorbachev wanted an end to SDI, which Reagan didn't agree to.

INF Treaty

- Diplomats continued the discussions from Reykjavik and came up with the INF Treaty.

- INF stood for Intermediate-Range Nuclear Forces – nuclear weapons with a 500–5500 km range.

- The INF Treaty got rid of all 500–5500 km nuclear missiles each superpower had – better than SALT 1.

- The INF Treaty was signed in December 1987.

Now try this

1. Suggest **two** reasons why Gorbachev was keen to improve relations with the USA.

2. Suggest **two** reasons why Reagan was prepared to reduce the numbers of nuclear weapons too.

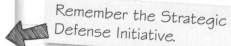

Remember the Strategic Defense Initiative.

The break-up of the Eastern Bloc

Gorbachev's reforms spread out from the USSR to Eastern Bloc countries, but not quite how he intended. Instead of making the Soviet system work better, the countries of the Eastern Bloc and many of the republics of the USSR wanted to become independent.

Brezhnev

Whenever something in an Eastern Bloc country makes it turn towards capitalism, the rest of the Eastern Bloc must make it turn back to communism.

Gorbachev

Eastern Bloc countries should be free to run themselves how they want and the USSR will not stop them.

Gorbachev scrapped the Brezhnev Doctrine because:

- He believed openness would make all Eastern Bloc countries better.
- The Eastern Bloc communist governments were only planning a little reform.
- The USSR had to improve trade relations with the West to rebuild its economy.
- Cost of troops and military hardware was crippling the USSR's economy.
- The West would only improve trade if repression was reduced.

There were many revolutions following *perestroika* and *glasnost*:

- Poland, June 1989
- Hungary, October 1989
- East Germany, November 1989
  - Fall of Berlin Wall, November 1989
  - Reunification of Germany, 1990
- Czechoslovakia, November 1989
- Bulgaria, December 1989
- Romania, December 1989.

Of all these revolutions, only the Romanian one was violent. The Warsaw Pact was ended in July 1991.

The fall of the Berlin Wall

Straight after the Hungarian revolution, people started leaving East Germany through Hungary. This forced the East German government to announce that East Germans could cross the Berlin border (9 November 1989). East Germans flooded into West Berlin and so the Berlin Wall fell.

Now try this

Give **three** reasons why Gorbachev's reforms led to the end of the Warsaw Pact.

The end of the Cold War

The break-up of the Eastern Bloc was followed by the break-up of the USSR. In December 1991, Gorbachev dissolved the USSR and resigned. The Cold War had ended.

The break-up of the USSR

Gorbachev's glasnost policies meant people could say what they thought. But perestroika only made the Soviet economy worse. This meant that living conditions for everyone got even worse than before. Many Soviet republics began to demand independence in 1990–91.

The August Coup, 1991

Gorbachev was very unpopular amongst Soviet hardliners. In August 1991, a group tried to take control and rescue the USSR.

Perestroika was ruining Soviet economy.

Glasnost had caused the break-up of Eastern Bloc.

Glasnost was causing USSR to break up.

Opposition to Gorbachev

Some of the republics hated each other and would start fighting.

Some of the republics could turn on Russian people living there.

The fall of the USSR

During the coup, Gorbachev was locked up in his holiday house. He could do nothing to stop it. But Boris Yeltsin led resistance to the coup in Moscow.

| The coup was defeated in a few days. Gorbachev returned to power. | → | But he looked weak while Yeltsin looked strong – the hero who had defended freedom. | → | Gorbachev tried to fix the USSR: republics could have more freedom. | → | But most republics wanted full independence. |

On 25 December 1991 Gorbachev dissolved the USSR and resigned.

Propaganda – It was hard for the USSR to 'sell' communism when capitalism seemed to work better and give people more.

Why did the USSR lose the Cold War?

Arms race – Catching up with the USA in the 1960s crippled the Soviet economy.

Afghan War – Huge cost of this long war was a major drain on the USSR's economy.

Freedom – The Eastern Bloc and Soviet republics only existed because of force and repression.

Economy – The Soviet economy was never as productive as that of the USA.

1970s–80s – The USSR's economy stagnated under Brezhnev while the USA forged ahead: e.g. while US firms developed personal computers, the USSR feared what Soviet people might do with their own computers: print and distribute anti-Soviet documents?

Now try this

Give **three** reasons to explain the end of the Cold War.

Six question types

In the Unit 1 exam you will answer questions from two sections: A and B. There are three questions in Section A: questions 1, 2 and 3, and you need to answer them all. There are also three questions in Section B: questions 4, 5 and 6. You need to answer all these too. You get a choice of two questions to answer for question 4 (**either** 4a **or** 4b) and a choice of three out of four events to explain in question 5.

Question 1

Question 1 is about **understanding** source material. The question gives you a source (Source A) and asks you to identify two pieces of information from the source.

- There is one mark for each reason.
- Only use reasons from the source, not your own knowledge.
- Only give two reasons as there are only 2 marks available.

Question 2

Question 2 is about **recalling** relevant information to answer a question. For example:

> Outline **two** reasons why President Reagan wanted to resume détente.

- One mark is for each factor (e.g. a reason for this example question): 2 marks in total.
- One mark is for additional detail to support each point: 2 marks in total.

Question 3

Question 3 is about assessing the **usefulness** of two sources. Question 3 will give you two sources (Sources A and B) and ask questions starting:

> How useful are Source A and B as evidence of the reasons for…

- 10 marks available.
- Consider what each source is useful for and consider their limitations too.
- Consider NOP: Nature, Origins, Purpose: what sort of source is it, who produced it, and why?
- Make sure you link your evaluation to the specific enquiry mentioned in the question.

Question 4

Question 4 will ask you to **describe** the key features of a major policy or an event. Question 4 may start like this:

> Describe the key features of the Cuban Missile Crisis.

- 6 marks available.
- You can score 3 marks for making three simple statements about key features.
- Higher marks require developed statements: you need to add supporting evidence.
- Be careful not to just tell the story of an event – select the key features.
- Choose **either** 4a **or** 4b, not both!

Question 5

Question 5 asks you to **explain** the importance of three out of four events listed in the question.

- 15 marks: 5 for each of the three events.
- No extra marks for doing all four!
- Make sure you **explain** how each event was important.
- Back up your answer with details.

Question 6

Question 6 is an extended writing question. It asks you to use your own knowledge to explain why something happened.

- 13 marks available, 3 are for SPaG.
- Aim for three causes as a minimum.
- Explain how each cause led to the outcome stated in the question.
- Explain which reason is most important.

The Weimar Republic 1918–23

You need to know about how the Weimar Republic was set up and what its early problems were.

Setting up the Weimar Republic and its constitution

After the Kaiser abdicated, uncertainty ensued. Friedrich Ebert put together a new government step-by-step, but it was built on shaky foundations and had major weaknesses.

The constitution had the following key features:

- proportional representation
- elections every four years
- the chancellor needed a majority in the Reichstag to pass laws
- the president could suspend the constitution and pass laws by decree.

The Weimar Republic

The constitution
Proportional representation meant that there were lots of small parties. Coalition governments were unstable and it was hard to get agreement when partners wanted different things. This led to difficulties in getting laws passed which meant that suspending the constitution was often the only way.

Bankruptcy (1923)
Germany spent all its gold reserves on the war, then lost wealth-making regions at Versailles, as well as having to pay reparations. By 1923 it was broke.

Attacks from left
The Spartacist uprising in January 1919 was defeated by the Weimar government with the help of Freikorps.

Treaty of Versailles
This was hated by Germans for harsh peace terms and Weimar politicians were blamed for signing it: they were branded as traitors. Germany had to pay reparations for war, which caused economic problems.

Problems for the Weimar Republic

French occupation of Ruhr
French troops occupied the Ruhr in January 1923 when Germany failed to pay reparations. German workers wrecked equipment, so the French couldn't make much money. The German economy was also wrecked.

Attacks from right: the Kapp Putsch
In March 1920, Kapp supporters seized power in Berlin while the army and police stood by. The Weimar government called on workers to strike and many did, so the Kapp Putsch failed.

Attacks from the right: the Munich Putsch
In November 1923, Adolf Hitler, leader of the Nazi Party, attempted to seize power in Bavaria (see page 23). The Putsch failed but Hitler's trial publicised his views.

Hyperinflation (1923)
The government printed money to pay reparations, wages and so on, which meant that money quickly became worthless. Living conditions declined.

Now try this

Which of the Republic's many problems would you identify as being economic problems?

Stresemann's successes at home and abroad

By 1929 the German economy was showing signs of recovering from the disastrous situation in 1923. There were also signs of increasing political stability. Stresemann's successes abroad led to the return of Germany to the international community.

Date	Measure	Effect / importance
November 1923	Stresemann introduced new currency – **Rentenmark**	• It stabilised the currency. • German people showed confidence in it.
1923–28	US loans	• Helped to pay reparations. • Greatly helped German industry.
1924	Rentenmark converted to **Reichsmark** (backed with gold)	• Gradually restored the value of German money.
1924	Stresemann negotiated the **Dawes Plan** with the USA	• Reorganised and reduced reparations. • French withdrew from the Ruhr.
1925	**Locarno Pact**	• Improved relations with Britain and France. • Guaranteed borders with Belgium, France and Italy.
1926	Stresemann negotiated German entry to the **League of Nations**	• Meant that Germany was recognised as a great power once again.
1928	**Kellogg–Briand Pact**	• Germany was one of 62 countries that agreed to settle disputes peacefully. • This wasn't a Stresemann initiative but meant better relations with the USA and France.
1929	**Young Plan**	• Set timescale and reduced reparations. • France agreed to leave the Rhineland early.

Evidence for recovery and remaining problems

- Politics became a bit more stable... ... but there were still plenty of short-lived coalition governments.

- Extremist parties were less popular... ... but they were still around.

- Unemployment fell... ... but it was still high compared to some countries.

- New roads, railways and homes were built... ... but this was almost completely due to US loans.

- By 1928, German industry was back to pre-war levels... ... but it slowed down after 1927 – and farming never picked up much at all.

- By 1930, Germany was a major exporter... ... but it was reliant on US loans and on the USA buying its exports.

- Germany was accepted by other countries again... ... but German nationalists hated the Dawes and Young plans.

Now try this

Explain the key features of Stresemann's role in the Republic's recovery.

Hitler and the Nazi Party 1919-23

Hitler's experiences in the First World War confirmed his views that Germany had a special destiny. Germany's defeat in the war was a terrible shock. Hitler joined what was to become the Nazi Party, full of determination to rescue Germany.

Was born in Austria but obsessed with everything German.

Wanted to be an artist but failed to get a place at art school.

Couldn't get a job so blamed Jews for controlling all the opportunities.

Blamed Jews and socialists for 'stabbing Germany in the back'.

Fought bravely in First World War and couldn't believe German defeat.

Hitler during the First World War.

Timeline

Hitler and the early DAP/NSDAP

1919 Hitler joined the DAP – German Workers' Party. Led by Anton Drexler

1920 Hitler was second in command of the DAP

1920 In August DAP changed its name to the National Socialist German Workers' Party: NSDAP, or Nazi for short

1921 Hitler took over control of the Nazi Party from Drexler

DAP/NSDAP policies

Treaty of Versailles must be scrapped

— ★ —

Germany must be allowed to expand into neighbouring countries – lebensraum

— ★ —

No German citizenship for Jews

— ★ —

Fight the Bolshevik menace

DAP/NSDAP: membership numbers

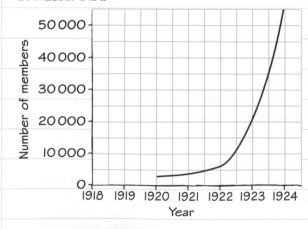

The Sturmabteilung

- Sturmabteilung means stormtroopers.
- Nazi Party's private army – the SA (nicknamed Brownshirts).
- Created by Hitler in 1921 for security and for fights with communists.
- Many right- and left-wing extremists had similar gangs.
- There were lots of unemployed ex-soldiers in Germany at this time.
- Hitler put Ernst Röhm in charge of the SA.

Now try this

The Nazi Party membership grew rapidly in 1923 after the French occupied the Ruhr. What was this event and why might it have made people join the NSDAP?

The years of struggle

The Nazis tried to take power in Munich by force, but their Putsch failed. Hitler realised they had to win power through elections. He reorganised the party to achieve this goal.

Why did the Nazis try to take power in Munich in 1923?

The unpopularity of the Weimar government among ordinary Germans increased in September 1923 when strikes in the Ruhr were called off and reparations to the French began.

The government of Bavaria was right-wing and didn't like the Weimar government – the Nazis thought the government would support them.

Former army leader General Ludendorff was close to Hitler, so the Nazis thought he could persuade the German army to support them.

The Nazis thought they were ready and Hitler was established as leader. They had about 55 000 supporters and the SA – most Nazi support was in Munich.

Consequences of the Putsch

The Putsch attempt failed because the Nazis failed to get support from the Munich government, the police or the army – and Hitler was imprisoned.

But Hitler's trial was a major propaganda victory which eventually led to election success in the 1930s. The judge was sympathetic and Hitler got a minimum sentence. Hitler dictated *Mein Kampf* while in prison, setting out the Nazi project.

Why were 1924–29 'lean years'?

Hitler re-launched the Nazi Party in 1924 and by 1929 it was very well organised. But 1924–29 had also been years when the Nazi Party lost support:

- The economy had improved – there was less unemployment.
- War hero Hindenburg was president of the Weimar Republic, which made it more popular.
- Stresemann was rebuilding Germany's international reputation.
- In the May 1928 elections the Nazis only won 12 seats in the Reichstag.

Reorganisation of the Nazi Party

1 The party was split into regions or *gaue* each of which was controlled by a *gauleiter*.

2 The party was given money by wealthy backers, e.g. companies such as Krupp.

3 The SA was expanded to 400 000. The SS was set up in 1925 as an elite bodyguard.

4 Party propaganda became more effective:
- it had a clear message and image
- close links with many newspapers (e.g. *Völkischer Beobachter*) allowed the spread of propaganda
- the Nazis used new technology such as radio and film.

Now try this

1. In the May 1928 general elections, the Nazis won only 2.6% of the national vote. Give **three** factors that limited their appeal.

2. Describe **three** ways in which the Nazis spread their propaganda message and **why** these methods were so successful.

The impact of the Great Depression

The Great Depression (1929–33) had a huge impact on Germany. Choking Germany's recovery, it massively increased the existing strains on the Weimar government.

Wall Street Crash, USA, October 1929

↓

The Great Depression
A worldwide economic recession triggered by the Wall Street Crash.

↓

Impact on Germany

German businesses
- They had to pay back loans to the USA and couldn't get new ones.
- They had to pay higher taxes to the government.
- The markets dried up, as few people in Germany or other countries had money to buy German goods.

German government
- It couldn't borrow money from the USA.
- It refused to print more money, so it had to increase taxes instead.
- Government workers lost their jobs and wages were reduced. The government also made cuts in the unemployment benefit.
- The government was blamed for depending on US loans.
- The coalition government already had its problems, as divided the government couldn't agree how to solve the crisis.

German people
- Millions of workers and farm labourers lost their jobs.
- Banks went bust and people lost their savings.
- Businesses collapsed, as did investments based on them.
- Young people were particularly badly affected by job losses.
- Many families suffered terrible poverty, as men couldn't find work and unemployment benefit had been reduced.
- In 1928, 0.8 million Germans were unemployed.
- By 1932, this had risen to 6 million.

Now try this

Give **three** reasons why the Great Depression helped the Nazi Party's rise to power.

Think about the problems caused by the Depression and the Weimar government's failure to solve them.

Who supported the Nazis 1929-33?

In May 1928, the Nazi Party only had 12 seats. By July 1932, the Nazis had 230 seats and were the biggest party in the Reichstag. How had this happened?

Strong propaganda
Hitler's personal appeal and a massive publicity effort with a clear message, which included: scrapping the Treaty of Versailles; beginning German expansion and fighting the Jews. Goebbels was very important in the propaganda effort.

Great Depression
Nazis offered hope and strong leadership.

SA as private army
Stronger than communists.

Some working-class support
The working class was the biggest group of voters. The Nazis were connected with jobs and images of a strong Germany but more workers supported the communists.

Reasons for Nazi Party success 1929-33

Support from women
The Nazis built support from some women with messages of the key role for women and the family in Germany's future.

Middle-class support
This group was hit hard by the Great Depression, felt let down by moderate parties and liked the Nazis' anticommunist message.

Farmers
The Nazis promised to protect farmers from communists.

Big business
The Nazis promised strong leadership and protection from communists. In return, big businesses supported the Nazis.

Impact of the Depression

The Great Depression was very important in building support for the Nazis.

- Unemployment hit the working class and the middle classes very hard.

- People lost faith in the moderate politicians – a succession of Weimar governments failed to tackle unemployment between 1929 and 1933.

- People turned to the extremist parties instead – communists on the left and the Nazis on the right.

- Workers liked the communists, but anyone with something to lose (such as businesses, farms or property) hated them. This meant that many middle class people voted for the Nazis to keep the communists out.

EXAM ALERT!

Questions about causation ask you to explain the reasons for an event. Often there will be several different reasons that interconnect. For example, the support of big business was an important reason for the Nazi Party's successes in 1929–33 because money funded propaganda and allowed the SA to be expanded.

Students have struggled with this topic in recent exams – **be prepared!**   Results Plus

Now try this

1 Why were the Nazis successful in getting support from farmers?

2 Why were the Nazis not so successful getting support from workers?

Hitler becomes chancellor

After the failure of the Munich Putsch in 1923, Hitler was determined to win power by legal, democratic means. By 1933, he was chancellor of the German government.

Timeline

Hitler becomes chancellor

May 1932 Chancellor Heinrich Brüning's popularity is very low; he depends on the president's decree. Hindenburg makes von Papen chancellor. under Article 48 of the Weimar Constitution

November 1932 Centre Party loses even more seats in another Reichstag election. The Nazis are still the largest party though they only win 196 seats this time

January 1933 Von Papen negotiates with Hitler so when von Schleicher resigns on 28 January due to lack of support, von Papen persuades Hindenburg to make Hitler chancellor

March 1932 Hindenburg beats Hitler in the presidential election but Hitler gains support

July 1932 Von Papen's Centre Party only has 68 seats so he depends on the president's decree – decides to hold Reichstag elections to gain more support but loses seats! The Nazis win 230 seats and become the largest party in the Reichstag but Hindenburg refuses to make Hitler chancellor

December 1932 Hindenburg is still ruling by decree. He removes von Papen and makes von Schleicher chancellor

Why did von Papen suggest Hitler for chancellor?

- The German government was always shaky because of coalitions. A party needed other parties' support in order to get laws passed.
- Hitler had the largest party, so von Papen wanted him on his side to give him support in the Reichstag.
- But Hitler's party was linked to a bunch of violent thugs: the SA fought pitched battles in the streets.
- So this was the plan that von Papen and the right-wingers came up with:

1 Get Nazi Party backing (230 seats in the Reichstag).

3 The Nazis depend on money from our friends, the big businesses, and we can cut that off any time we need to.

2 The Nazis won't remain this popular for long, so then they'll do as we say.

4 Make Hitler the chancellor but we will control him to get what we want.

Now try this

1. Explain the steps that made Hitler the German chancellor in January 1933.

2. Explain **why** von Papen and Hindenburg thought they would be able to control Hitler as chancellor.

Removing the opposition

The Nazis were very effective at taking control of Germany and removing opposition. They used **legal methods** (the March 1933 election, the Enabling Act), **party organisation** (propaganda got the votes in, party contacts got huge donations from business) and **illegal methods** (intimidation and violence).

The Reichstag fire

On 27 February 1933, the Reichstag building was burned down. A Dutch communist, Marinus van der Lubbe, confessed. Thousands of communists were arrested on 8 February. Hitler persuaded Hindenburg to declare a state of emergency and call an election.

The Nazis won 288 seats, and made deals to get the two-thirds majority needed to change the constitution.

The Enabling Act in March 1933 gave Hitler the power to make whatever laws he wanted without Reichstag approval for four years.

People could be arrested and held without trial (suspension of Habeas Corpus).

Any house could be searched and belongings confiscated (Germany became a police state).

Hitler used the powers given to him by the Enabling Act to create a one-party state in Germany. This policy was called Gleichschaltung or 'co-ordination'.

Censorship of the press and Ministry of Propaganda established.

What happened after the Enabling Act

People were prevented from organising into groups that might challenge the Nazis.

Other political parties banned (July 1933: Law against the Formation of Parties).

Regional parliaments closed down (January 1934).

Trade unions were banned (and replaced by the German Labour Front) and strikes were made illegal (May 1933).

The Night of the Long Knives

Röhm (SA leader) challenged Hitler because he wanted the Nazis to be less about big business and more about the workers. The SS got rid of this opposition: they shot Röhm and about 400 other opponents (30 June 1934).

The death of Hindenburg

President Hindenburg died in August 1934. Hitler declared himself Führer, added all the powers of president to the chancellor's role, and made every soldier swear an oath to him personally. Nazi propaganda ensured 90% of voters agreed that Hitler should be Führer.

Now try this

1   Explain how Hitler got the Enabling Act passed.

2   Why was the Enabling Act so significant in the development of Hitler's dictatorship?

The Nazi police state

A police state is when a government uses the police to control everyone's lives. The Nazis used the SS and the Gestapo to do this. Anyone the Nazis didn't like could disappear, at any time.

Features of the Nazi police state

1 **New laws** were passed which made it a crime to do things such as listen to a foreign radio station, say anything against Hitler or tell an anti-Nazi joke.

2 The **SS** became the main feature of the police state. They arrested people who were accused of breaking the new laws or opponents of the Nazis. They called it taking into 'protective custody'.

3 The **Gestapo** were the secret police. They used lots of methods (e.g. reading mail, listening in on phone calls) to spy on people.

4 **Wardens** were given about 40 households each to spy on and report any suspicious behaviour.

5 People were encouraged to be **informers** and spy on their friends and family.

6 **Law courts** were also under total Nazi control. There was no trial by jury. All judges took an oath of loyalty to Hitler.

7 **Concentration camps** were where many prisoners were taken – e.g. Dachau (the first camp to open in 1933).

8 **Totalitarian regime:** central government in control of every aspect of the country.

Targets for the police state

The Nazis used their police state to get rid of opponents and intimidate everyone else.

Communists and other political opponents.

Christians – the Nazis had no time for kindness, forgiveness and peacefulness. If Christians didn't support the Nazis, they became targets.

Undesirables – these were people the Nazis thought didn't deserve to be in German society. They could be anyone, especially Jews, communists, gay people, and many others. Many were placed in concentration camps such as Dachau and Buchenwald.

The Churches

- A Nazi Concordat with the Pope in 1933 allowed German Catholics to worship if their bishops agreed to support the Nazis.

- But the Nazis went back on their promise: they harassed priests, closed Church schools and banned Catholic youth organisations.

- Some Protestants in the Confessional Church backed Hitler, forming the Reich Church under Ludwig Muller.

- But some Protestants opposed Hitler and were sent to concentration camps, such as Martin Niemöller and Dietrich Bonhoeffer.

Now try this

1 Describe how the Gestapo helped the Nazis to control Germany.

2 Describe how the law courts helped the Nazis to control Germany.

Controlling and influencing attitudes

Hitler wanted to use propaganda and censorship as a means of creating a generation of people loyal to the Nazi regime and its values.

Definitions

Censorship is when the government controls what people see, hear and read.

Propaganda is information given out to spread ideas or points of view.

Goebbels

Played a central role as Nazi Minister of Enlightenment and Propaganda. He was a master at spreading Nazi ideas in a subtle as well as an unsubtle way. He essentially controlled newspapers, the radio, book publishing, films and the arts.

Public burning of books by Jewish writers or books that disagreed with Nazi views.

Reich Chamber of Culture was set up in 1933. Only members of the Chamber were allowed to publish or perform their work.

'Decadent' art and culture banned by the regime including modern styles of art and jazz.

Methods of censorship

Only short-range radios were made, as they couldn't receive foreign stations.

Books could only be published with the government's permission.

Newspapers that opposed the Nazis were shut down.

Radio producers, playwrights, academics, film-makers and newspapers were told what to produce by the Nazis.

Methods of propaganda

posters

radio

cinema

rallies

plays

art

education

sport

slogans

Ein Volk, ein Reich, ein Führer!

Hitler's image as leader was a key feature of Nazi propaganda. The slogan reads: One People, One Nation, One Leader!

Now try this

1 What can you learn from the propaganda poster on this page about the message the Nazis wanted to give the German people?

2 Why did the Nazis encourage the mass production of cheap radios for the German market?

Nazi policies towards the young and women

The Nazis had strong views about how German society should be. Once they had control of Germany, they introduced policies to make those views into reality.

Young people

- The Nazis wanted control over children to make them into good Nazi citizens.
- Only Nazi youth groups were allowed; other youth groups (e.g. political and Church ones) were closed down.

At school, children studied subjects that glorified Nazi views, including the following:

- Race studies taught about Aryan superiority and Nazi views on Jews.
- There was a lot of PE: the Nazis wanted fit and healthy young people.
- Boys were trained for work and military roles. Girls were trained to be housewives and mothers.

Youth groups

- Little Fellows (boys 6–10)
- Young German Folk (boys 10–14)
- Young Girls (girls 10–14)
- Hitler Youth (boys 14–18)
- League of German Maidens (girls 14–18)
- Eight million children were members of these groups by 1939.

You will do well to remember that there were problems with these groups and not everyone liked them. For example:

- Some parents didn't like the groups for encouraging children to spy.
- A few young people refused to attend and some even joined rebel groups such as the Edelweiss Pirates.

Nazi policies for women

- The Nazis said women had a vital role for Germany but a different one from men, one defined by the 3Ks – kinder, küche, kirche (children, kitchen, church).
- Many professional women (doctors, lawyers, teachers) lost their jobs and first choice of jobs was given to men.
- The 1933 Law for the Encouragement of Marriage lent couples money when they married if the wife left work. For each child they had they were let off a quarter of this loan.
- The German Women's Enterprise gave women medals for having children (bronze for 4–5 children, silver for 6–7, gold for over 8), as well as classes and radio programmes on household topics.

How successful were Nazi policies?

- The number of married women in employment fell (1933–36) but then rose again when male workers left for war.
- The number of marriages and the birth rate increased – but this may have been due to the improving economy rather than Nazi policies.
- Few women had more than two children.
- The German Women's Enterprise had 6 million members.
- Many employers chose to employ women because women were paid two-thirds of a man's wage.

Now try this

How successful were the Nazis' policies for young people and women?

(a) Outline **three** points showing success.

(b) Outline **three** points suggesting the policies did not work that well.

Employment and the standard of living

The Nazis needed the economy to serve their needs too, in order to rebuild Germany to be a great power again. They also needed a solution to unemployment and to raise standards of living for the German people.

 DAF

German Labour Front
Set working hours.
Set rates of pay.
Made sure workers did what state needed.
Made sure employers also did what state needed.

 RAD

National Labour Service
Got unemployed working.
Compulsory from 1935 for all young men.
Army-style work and living conditions.
Public works – e.g. building 7000 miles of autobahn by 1939.

3 Rearmament

The Nazis wanted to rebuild German military power.
Military spending rose from 3.5 billion marks (1933) to 26 billion marks (1939).
Hitler wanted Germany to be ready for war.
Economy refocused on the goal of supplying the military.
Boost for factories making weapons, uniforms, etc.
Helped reduce unemployment and boosted the economy.

Arguments **for** Nazi success in raising living standards	Arguments **against** Nazi success in raising living standards
👍 In 1933, there were 4.8 million unemployed – this went down to 0.5 million in 1938.	👎 People had to work longer hours.
👍 Wages rose and people could afford consumer goods.	👎 The Nazis reduced unemployment by shifting men into the military, or pushing them into RAD, by stopping women from working, also invisible unemployment: pushing Jews and former communists out of jobs.
👍 Car ownership increased x 3 in the 1930s.	
👍 SdA (Beauty of Labour): improved working conditions.	👎 Although wages rose, so did prices – became more expensive to buy things.
👍 KdF (Strength through Joy): holidays and leisure activities for workers.	👎 Standards of living were so low in the Great Depression that they were bound to rise once the Depression was over.
👍 Lots of public support for Nazis because of better living standards.	👎 Overspending on the military meant that Germany would soon start to run out of money.

Now try this

Answer this question using the arguments on this page and your own knowledge:

Was rearmament the most important reason for the fall in unemployment in Germany between 1933 and 1939?

EXAM ALERT!

Make sure you understand what is meant by 'standard of living'.

Students have struggled with this topic in recent exams – **be prepared!**

 ResultsPlus

Nazi persecution

Nazi Germany was only for some people. The Nazis hated Jews in particular but also persecuted Gypsies and wanted to rid society of any groups they saw as 'weak' influences, which included disabled people, gay people, alcoholics, pacifists and mentally ill people.

Timeline

Jewish persecution

1935 Jews banned from the army and public places like restaurants

1936 Jews banned or restricted from being teachers, nurses, dentists, vets and accountants

1939 April All Jews to be evicted from their homes and moved to ghettos (easily controlled city areas) – thousands died from disease and starvation

1933 Boycotts of Jewish shops, Jews banned from government jobs and from inheriting land

1935 Nuremburg Laws – deny Jews German citizenship (so they lose the right to vote). Jews banned from marrying Aryans

1938 March Jews have to register their property
July All Jews to carry identity cards
Nov Kristallnacht – following an attack by a Polish Jew on a German citizen, the Nazis encouraged widespread anti-Jewish riots and attacks on Jews

Why

Why did the German people let the persecution happen?
- Long-standing distrust of Jews (this was common across Europe).
- Nazi anti-Semitic propaganda.
- Fear of the Gestapo and SS.

Kristallnacht 1938

- Jewish shops and synagogues set on fire or smashed up.
- 20 000 Jews arrested, about 100 killed.
- Jewish community blamed for the attack and ordered to pay a fine and pay for damage to their own property.
- Jews barred from owning businesses.

Persecution of other minorities

Nazis believed some races were superior to others:

Aryans at the top: white, blond, blue-eyed, fit and healthy.

↓

Lesser races – such as Slavs.

↓

Untermenschen (sub-humans) – such as Africans.

↓

Lebensunwertes (not worthy of life) – Jews and Gypsies.

The Nazis believed inferior races should be removed from German society because they polluted it.

The disabled

Nazis also persecuted people with physical and mental disabilities because they thought that they would weaken German society.

- Nazis said disabled babies should be allowed to die.
- Disabled people and other 'weak' people should be sterilised.

Gypsies

Gypsies were persecuted like Jews: the Nuremburg Laws prohibited marriage with Aryans and from April 1939, Gypsies were rounded up into ghettos.

Now try this

Outline the changes that happened in Nazi persecution of the Jews between 1933 and 1939.

Social inequality in Russia, 1914

Russia in 1917 was a country divided between modernisation and old traditions. The ruler of Russia, Tsar Nicholas II, was not willing to give up any power and this set the scene for revolution.

Nicholas II – a Tsar with problems

Ruler of 126 million people, around 125 million of whom were very poor.

Nicholas II had never wanted to be Tsar and found it hard to make decisions.

Nicholas and his wife relied on a strange, scandalous 'holy man' called Rasputin, who was very unpopular.

Ruler of an enormous country with very few railways and roads that turned to mud in spring.

The Tsar was believed to be appointed by God as sole ruler of Russia – so he should be infallible (unable to make mistakes).

Ruler of many nationalities (less than half his subjects spoke Russian), but Russians were always put first.

A few Russians were getting richer – but they wanted to be involved in running Russia.

Rapid urbanisation in a few big cities but terrible living conditions for workers.

Nicholas II

Most of the population were peasants – almost all without enough land to live on, most in debt to their landlords.

Opposition groups

While many Russians supported the Tsar and the old ways of doing things, there were two main groups who wanted change.

Constitutionalists were middle-class Russians who wanted to share power with the Tsar, more like the UK system. Examples included:
- Kadets
- Octobrists.

Revolutionaries wanted to overthrow Tsarism and have Russia run by the peasants or by the workers. Examples:
- Social Revolutionaries (SRs) believed in peasant-led revolution.
- Social Democrats (SDs) believed in worker-led revolution.

Soviets wanted reforms to help ordinary workers.

The Tsar's broken promises

Nicholas II had clung on to power after a revolution in 1905 by making promises:
- A Duma (parliament) would share the job of running Russia.
- Political parties would be allowed – these had been illegal.
- Trade unions would help workers improve working conditions (also previously illegal).

But once the trouble died down, he went back on his promises. He had no intention of sharing his power.

The Bolsheviks were a group of SDs who believed Russia was ready for a workers' revolution.

Now try this

Look at the problems facing Tsar Nicholas II. Which **three** do you think were the most serious threats to his rule?

The impact of the First World War

Although the First World War was very popular in Russia at first, it went badly wrong very quickly. The war made all of Russia's problems even worse, and opposition to the Tsar reached new heights.

Events leading to the revolution

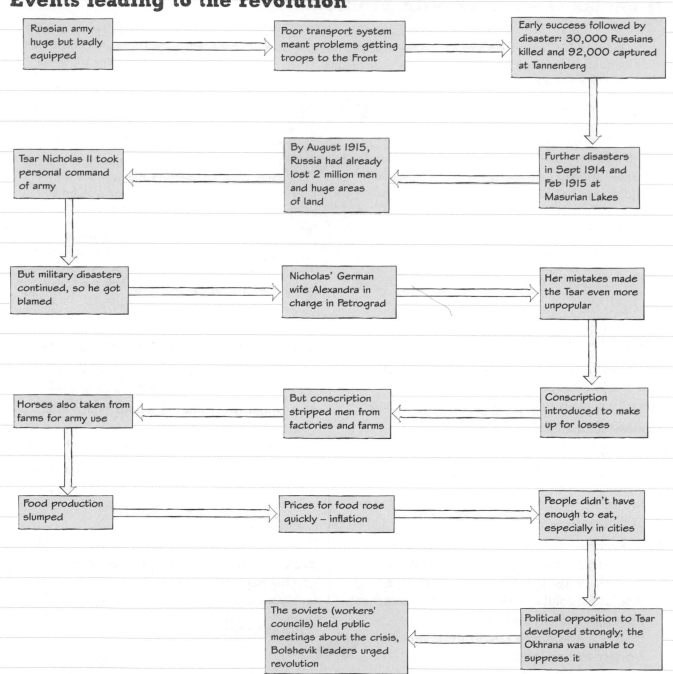

| Russian army huge but badly equipped | → | Poor transport system meant problems getting troops to the Front | → | Early success followed by disaster: 30,000 Russians killed and 92,000 captured at Tannenberg |

Tsar Nicholas II took personal command of army ← By August 1915, Russia had already lost 2 million men and huge areas of land ← Further disasters in Sept 1914 and Feb 1915 at Masurian Lakes

But military disasters continued, so he got blamed → Nicholas' German wife Alexandra in charge in Petrograd → Her mistakes made the Tsar even more unpopular

Horses also taken from farms for army use ← But conscription stripped men from factories and farms ← Conscription introduced to make up for losses

Food production slumped → Prices for food rose quickly – inflation → People didn't have enough to eat, especially in cities

The soviets (workers' councils) held public meetings about the crisis, Bolshevik leaders urged revolution ← Political opposition to Tsar developed strongly; the Okhrana was unable to suppress it

Now try this

1   Describe **two** problems with Russia's army that help explain why it was repeatedly defeated by the Germans.

2   Explain why many Russians blamed the Tsar directly for Russia's disastrous losses in the war.

The fall of the Tsar

The war led to the February 1917 Revolution – the first revolution of 1917. Left without support from the Duma or the army, the Tsar was forced to abdicate.

The February 1917 Revolution

- The war re-energised opposition.
- The **soviets** stirred up the workers.
- Opponents of Tsarism openly criticised the Tsar and his failures.
- Food shortages led to rationing being announced in Petrograd.
- Strikes spread rapidly and the police could not stop them.
- Tsar Nicholas II ordered the strikes to be put down by force on 26 February.
- By 27 February, the army had mutinied and had joined the revolution.

The Provisional Government

- Some people looked to the Petrograd Soviet for leadership, others to the Duma (parliament).
- The revolution had come so quickly that the Bolsheviks weren't ready for it – they missed their chance for power.
- 2 March 1917: 12 Duma representatives set up a Provisional Government, with the backing of the soviets.
- The Provisional Government was to look after Russia until a new democratic government system was worked out.
- 15 March 1917: the Tsar was forced to abdicate and he was arrested.

The Petrograd Soviet agreed to support the new government if **eight principles** were followed:

1 Amnesty for all political prisoners.

2 Freedom of speech, freedom of assembly, right to strike.

3 No privileges of class, religion or nationality.

4 Elections for a Constituent Assembly.

5 Elected people's militia to replace all police units.

6 Local government to be elected.

7 Military units that took part in the revolution to stay together, keep weapons and not be sent to the front.

8 Off-duty soldiers to have same rights as citizens.

Soviet Order No. 1:

The army must obey the Provisional Government, except where the orders contradict those of the Petrograd Soviet.

The Petrograd Soviet

Now try this

1 Which of these terms do you think best describes the February Revolution and **why**?

   ☐ Inevitable   ☐ Planned   ☐ Spontaneous

2 Explain the meaning of the term 'soviet'.

Provisional Government problems

The Provisional Government was not solving Russia's many problems quickly. The Bolsheviks, led by Lenin, rapidly became very popular with the workers. Lenin was an inspirational leader who returned to Russia in April 1917 with help from the German government.

Weaknesses of the Provisional Government

Failed to improve military position – June 1917 offensive was a failure.

Couldn't end the war without letting down Russia's important allies, Britain and France.

Couldn't give peasants more land without upsetting landlords.

Failed to improve the economy – there was no quick way to solve shortages or improve conditions.

Depended on the support of the Petrograd Soviet and the army – very weak position. The Bolsheviks had their own Red Guard force: armed workers.

More democracy and free speech meant more criticism of the government (for instance, by June 1917 there were 41 different Bolshevik newspapers).

The 'July Days'

More uprisings happened in Petrograd in July 1917 – against the war, bread rationing (introduced March 1917) and the Provisional Government.

⬇

The Bolsheviks stepped in to lead the demonstrations.

⬇

But the Provisional Government sent troops to put down the demonstrations. Hundreds of people were killed.

⬇

The Bolshevik leaders had to go into hiding to escape arrest. Red Guards were imprisoned and Lenin fled to Finland.

Kerensky's bad decisions

1 Army chief Kornilov wanted to break the power of the soviets. Kornilov marched on Petrograd.

2 Provisional Government leader Kerensky freed the Red Guards and armed them to defend Petrograd.

3 Petrograd Soviet activists, led by Bolsheviks, met Kornilov's soldiers and convinced them to give up.

4 The Bolsheviks now had access to weapons and support among soldiers and sailors based in Petrograd.

5 The Bolsheviks were keen to blame Kerensky for the affair, who they accused of encouraging Kornilov. This further reduced his support, placing him in a very weak position.

Reasons why Bolshevik power grew

- As the Provisional Government failed to deliver, the Bolsheviks seemed to have more to offer.
- The Bolsheviks' very clear messages targeted Provisional Government failures.
- Lenin was a great organiser and communicator – his ideas were set out in his April Thesis.
- Trotsky helped set up Red Guards and was a leader in the Petrograd Soviet.
- The Bolsheviks' role in defending Petrograd from Kornilov.

Now try this

One Bolshevik slogan was 'Peace, Land, Bread'. Explain what the **three** words referred to and why they were a powerful slogan for Russia in 1917.

The October Revolution

The Bolsheviks had missed their chance in the February Revolution and the July Days hadn't been organised. Lenin decided the Bolsheviks must act fast or lose their chance completely. In hiding in Finland after the July Days, Lenin weighed up the Bolsheviks' chances of taking power.

The army is very dissatisfied and full of Bolshevik supporters.

The Provisional Government is divided and ineffective.

The December 1917 election of Constituent Assembly and growth of democracy in Russia could replace the soviets, making us redundant.

Lenin

The peasants believe the Bolsheviks will give them land.

The Bolsheviks are the only party that has a clear plan of what to do.

Maybe another general like Kornilov will try to restore Tsarism.

The Bolsheviks should act now! We should organise and lead an armed insurrection.

Timeline

The October Revolution (1917)

10 Oct Lenin back in Petrograd

24 Oct Kerensky shuts down Bolshevik newspapers and cuts off phone line to Bolshevik HQ

25 Oct Bolsheviks surround the Winter Palace, trapping most of the Provisional Government inside (Kerensky escapes). The Congress of Soviets argues about the Bolshevik take-over. Everyone who disagrees with it walks out

8 Oct Trotsky chair of Petrograd Soviet and ran its Military Revolutionary Committee (MRC)

21 Oct Most of Petrograd's armed forces side with Trotsky's MRC

24 Oct Lenin agrees to start the insurrection. Bolsheviks set off to capture key Petrograd locations

26 Oct The Congress of Soviets meets again and hands power to the Council of People's Commissars (CPC) – Lenin is elected chairman with Trotsky in charge of foreign affairs

Why was the October Revolution successful?

Lenin was single-minded with a clear plan of attack.

Lenin made sure the Bolsheviks were in charge and not any other revolutionary group.

Kerensky didn't take the Bolshevik threat seriously after the July Days.

Kerensky didn't disband the Red Guards after the Kornilov affair.

The Provisional Government had become very unpopular and no one stood up to defend it.

Trotsky was an amazing planner who formed Red Guards into an effective fighting force.

Now try this

Answer this question using the arguments on this page and your own knowledge:

Was the unpopularity of the Provisional Government the most important reason for the October 1917 Revolution?

Remember that whatever conclusion you come to when answering questions like the one here, you need to be able to explain how and why you have come to the conclusion. It may be helpful to draw a flowchart or spider diagram to organise your thoughts.

Bolsheviks in control?

The Bolsheviks passed decrees to live up to their promises, but the results of the Constituent Assembly elections threatened Bolshevik control.

Three key decrees

Once the Bolsheviks were in power, they immediately set out three decrees:

1 The Peace Decree – Russia would negotiate for peace with Germany.

2 The Land Decree – All land owned by the state, the Church and landlords to be given to the peasants (through land committees).

3 The Workers' Decree – Workers given control of factories, maximum 8-hour working day.

Other measures

- Power was given to local soviets to run all town and countryside districts.
- Elections for the Constituent Assembly were to be held on 12 November.
- Capital punishment was abolished.

The Treaty of Brest-Litovsk

Trotsky negotiated this with the Germans to get Russia out of the First World War. Negotiations began on 22 December 1917 and the treaty was signed on 3 March 1918. The Germans had nearly defeated Russia and set extremely harsh terms for peace. Russia lost massive amounts of territory, e.g. Ukraine and Baltic provinces, 80% of its coalmines, 50% of its industry, 26% of its railways, 26% of its population and 27% of its farmland.

THE DAILY NEWS

Constituent Assembly Elections Shock!

Bolshevik power under threat?
The Bolsheviks expected to win the elections of 12 November 1917 for the democratic Constituent Assembly. After all, the Bolshevik decrees had made good on their promises for Peace, Land and Bread...

Shock poll upset
But in a shock result, it was the peasants' favourite party, the Social Revolutionaries, who came out top. With 370 deputies, the SRs are way ahead of the Bolsheviks, who got 170 deputies in the new Assembly.

SR backing doubtful
Will the SRs back the Bolsheviks' bold policies? We'll see when the Constituent Assembly meets for the first time on 5 January 1918!

Constituent Assembly, 5 January 1918

The SRs and other parties blocked the Bolsheviks' decrees, saying they were not proper laws. There was also alarm over the Treaty of Brest-Litovsk. Lenin ordered the Red Guards to shut down the Constituent Assembly. It never reopened. Democracy didn't work for the Bolsheviks!

The Red Terror

In September 1918, the Council of People's Commissars decreed that the Cheka (secret police) can imprison and shoot enemies of the Revolution.

Now try this

1. Why do you think the Social Revolutionaries did so well in the elections for the Constituent Assembly?

2. Suggest **two** reasons why the Bolsheviks agreed to such harsh terms in the Treaty of Brest-Litovsk.

The civil war

Lenin knew that he would have to fight to keep control of Russia, but the experience of the civil war transformed the Bolsheviks' attitude to ruling Russia. The Bolsheviks formed the Red Army and were opposed by the Whites, an alliance of anti-Bolshevik groups.

Enemies on all sides

- Kerensky intended to bring back the Provisional Government.

- Kornilov and others wanted to bring back the Tsar.

- Russia's First World War allies were furious that Russia had given in to Germany.

- Other forces, such as Kolchak in Siberia and the Czech Legion.

By 22 October 1919, the White armies had reached Petrograd and Bolshevik defeat was almost certain.

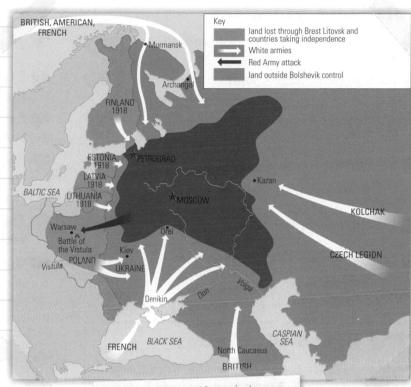

Key
land lost through Brest Litovsk and countries taking independence
White armies
Red Army attack
land outside Bolshevik control

Russia during the civil war.

Trotsky set up the Red Army and ran it brilliantly.

Bolshevik secret police (Cheka) crushed political opposition within Russia.

The Reds controlled the centre ground around Moscow which was easier to organise. This gave them control of the railway network which meant that they could quickly move troops to meet attacks from the Whites.

Trotsky was an inspirational and ruthless war leader. This meant that Bolshevik troops were well disciplined and fought effectively.

The Bolsheviks inherited most of Russia's weapons and heavy industry. This gave them an advantage over their opponents.

How did the Bolsheviks win?

White leaders treated their troops badly.

White armies were not well co-ordinated and disagreed on aims. Some wanted to restore the monarchy in Russia. Others wanted to turn Russia into a military dictatorship.

War Communism meant that soldiers had sufficient food and weapons to fight the war even if it also destroyed the economy.

The end of the First World War meant that the Allies stopped supporting the White armies.

Now try this

1 Explain how the Cheka helped the Bolsheviks keep hold of power in Russia.

2 Explain how War Communism helped the Bolsheviks keep hold of power.

Creating a new society

War Communism began in May 1918. It was necessary to win the civil war but it was a long way from the new society the Bolsheviks had promised – and it was ruining Russia. The Bolsheviks had to bring in their New Economic Policy (NEP) or risk losing everything.

Bolshevik promises

👍 The right to free speech and a free press.

👍 All power to the soviets.

👍 Abolition of capital punishment.

👍 An end to food shortages.

👍 Land to the peasants.

👍 Improving workers' rights and conditions.

War Communism in reality

👎 The Cheka and the Red Terror.

👎 State control of factories to meet the needs of the Red Army.

👎 Executions to control the army and the people.

👎 Food was requisitioned to feed the army so some areas suffered famine.

👎 The state took all peasants' crops without payment.

👎 Banning strikes and arresting strikers.

The Kronstadt Mutiny

In March 1921 sailors from the Kronstadt naval base, near Petrograd, issued demands for a 'third revolution'. Among other things they called for:

- re-election of all soviets (because the current soviets were stuffed with Bolsheviks)
- freedom of speech and a free press for all socialist groups, not just the Bolsheviks
- freedom for all socialist political prisoners
- no more Bolshevik stooges in the army or in factories
- freedom for the peasants to do what they want with their farms.

The mutiny was crushed by Red Army troops, but it had a big impact on the Bolsheviks.

New Economic Policy (NEP)

The NEP turned back the clock on the socialist revolution:

- Workers were paid wages.
- Peasants could sell their crops (with a 10% tax to the state).
- Factories with fewer than 20 workers could be run privately (anything bigger remained owned by the state).
- These private factories could sell their products for profit.
- Anyone could set up a shop and sell things for profit.

The NEP worked. Both agricultural and industrial production went up. The economy improved and people had enough to live on again.

Now try this

Explain the key differences between War Communism and the NEP.

A socialist society has no private ownership. The workers own everything in common.

Stalin's struggle for power

Trotsky was the most likely person to take over after Lenin's death. But Stalin built up a power base in the Party and set his rivals for the leadership against each other. Trotsky's weaknesses and mistakes meant he was pushed out.

Name: Trotsky

The mastermind behind the October Revolution and civil war victory.

Believed in world revolution (i.e. that there could not be a true socialist society until the whole world was socialist).

Weaknesses and mistakes

- Put his work first and didn't care whom he upset.
- His role as Commissar for War meant that many people in the Party feared that he might turn Russia into a military dictatorship.
- Hated the way that bureaucrats were taking over the Party.
- Missed Lenin's funeral, criticised Lenin after his death.
- Lacked Stalin's network of supporters inside the Party.

Name: Stalin

Not a key leader in the October Revolution or civil war but an efficient bureaucrat and administrator.

Believed in 'socialism in one country', i.e. that the Soviet Union was strong enough to survive on its own.

Achievements and characteristics

- Became General Secretary of the Communist Party in 1922.
- Used his position to promote people in the Party who supported him.
- Used his supporters to remove his rivals. By 1929 he had complete control of the Party.
- Very ambitious and extremely suspicious.

Getting rid of Trotsky

Stalin worked with other Party leaders (and rivals), Kamenev and Zinoviev, to push Trotsky out. They spread rumours about him. Stalin made sure he promoted only Party members who opposed Trotsky.

Timeline

Trotsky's fate

1926 Trotsky was expelled from Party leadership

1927 Trotsky was expelled from the Party

1929 Trotsky was exiled from USSR

1940 Trotsky was assassinated on Stalin's orders

Getting rid of other rivals

Stalin then used the same methods against his other rivals – such as Kamenev and Zinoviev – as he had against Trotsky.

- Used his control of the Party to build up supporters.
- Spread rumours about rivals betraying the Communist Party.
- Got the Party to remove rivals.

Stalin set his rivals against each other and they failed to band together against him.

The end of the power struggle meant that by 1929 the Soviet Union had turned into a dictatorship with Stalin firmly in power.

Now try this

Explain how Stalin used his position as General Secretary of the Communist Party to get rid of his rivals for power.

Terror in the 1930s

Stalin's determination to get rid of any rivals kept spreading, until the whole Soviet Union was purged of anyone who might be an 'enemy of the people'.

Kirov's assassination

Stalin's policies in farming and industry caused big problems in the Soviet Union. By the 1930s, the Party started to criticise Stalin. Even Sergei Kirov, one of Stalin's closest allies, called for a change in policy, and Stalin became very suspicious. He thought Kirov wanted to take the leadership from him.

Kirov was assassinated in December 1934. Stalin then claimed that a huge conspiracy, led by Trotsky, was responsible.

After Kirov's death, Stalin purged the Party of anyone who might challenge his leadership. These purges spread to the whole of Soviet society.

Stalin used existing Bolshevik systems for his purges:

- **Secret police** – Stalin used the OGPU, a new version of the Cheka (later known as the NKVD and then the KGB).
- **Gulags** – these labour camps were a new version of the Bolsheviks' prison camps. The secret police used terror to get confessions. People were arrested in the middle of the night, tortured, deprived of sleep, their families and friends threatened, until they signed confessions to made-up crimes.
- **Terror** – Stalin's Great Terror was similar to the climate of fear in the civil war.

These systems were descendants of Tsarist secret police and labour camps, too.

Timeline

The Great Terror

1936 16 senior party members were made to confess to crimes in show trials: including Kamenev and Zinoviev

1937 17 more party rivals were put on trial: all found guilty and 13 shot

1938 21 party members found guilty and executed or sent to camps

1937–38 Purge spread to Red Army as Stalin was worried about a military takeover

1938 Purge spread to NKVD (secret police), as they knew too much about the purges

By the end of the **1930s**, everyone was in danger. 20 million Russians were sent to the gulags and around half died there

The impact of the Great Terror

1 A climate of fear existed, so no one took any risks or challenged official policies. Everyone watched what they said for fear of informers.

2 Skilled people in industry, the arts, teaching, medicine and similar professions were most likely to be purged. The USSR lost millions of talented people in these years.

3 The Red Army lost many of its best generals (imprisoned or executed), which made the USSR more vulnerable to military attack by the Nazis in 1941.

4 Show trials made people frightened that there could be traitors everywhere, and more people were likely to put their trust in Stalin's leadership.

Now try this

Explain the effects of the purges.

Censorship and propaganda

Stalin, now dictator of the USSR, strengthened his control over the Soviet Union by censoring anything negative about the state and using propaganda to flood the USSR with positive images of himself and communism. Stalin established his own **personality cult**.

Definitions

Censorship is when the state controls what people see, hear and read. In the USSR the state controlled all media, even art and music.

Propaganda is information given out to spread ideas or points of view.

Methods of propaganda

Propaganda films were shown all over Russia, giving a false picture of how well everything was going.

The five-year plans for the economy were promoted.

Records from the past were changed: for example, photos featuring Trotsky and Lenin were altered to show only Lenin.

Posters, banners and signs praised Stalin and the Communist Party.

Soviet propaganda

'Social realist' art depicted a glorious USSR, filled with happy people building socialism together.

Artists, writers, film-makers, singers and so on were all employed by the state and commissioned to create things glorifying the Soviet Union.

School textbooks had to be approved by the state and teachers who did not follow the state line were likely to be purged.

The cults of Lenin and Stalin – Lenin was portrayed like a saint, everything he ever did being glorified and praised. Similarly Stalin's supporters said that Stalin was all-wise and all-powerful.

The 1936 Constitution

👍 It replaced the Congress of Soviets with the Supreme Soviet of the USSR.

👍 Instead of only some people being allowed to vote, everyone was allowed.

👍 Instead of voting being open, it was done in secret so no one could see how you voted.

👍 It guaranteed workers' rights to holidays, health care, housing, education and other benefits.

👍 It gave the 15 republics of the USSR the same rights as Russia.

However, the 1936 Constitution was mostly propaganda:

👎 People could all vote but there was only one party to vote for.

👎 Workers had lots of rights but these rights could all be ignored by the secret police.

👎 The activities of all the republics of the USSR were closely controlled from Moscow by the Communist Party.

👎 Stalin ignored the Constitution and ran the USSR as a dictatorship.

Now try this

Explain how the cult of Lenin helped to maintain Stalin's control over the USSR.

 Remember that Stalin portrayed himself as Lenin's chosen successor – even though he wasn't!

Collectivisation

Collectivisation was Stalin's agricultural policy, which tried to transform peasant agriculture into a communist food production system.

Peasant system

- Peasants own the land they farm (since 1917) and everything it produces.
- Village elders work out what crops to sow and when to sow them, based on tradition.
- Village elders allocate land to families according to how much they can farm.
- Big jobs like harvesting and ploughing are done as a community.
- Old fashioned, inefficient methods, no modern machinery.
- Most produce is used to feed the family – anything extra is stored or sold.

2 Collective farm system

- The state owns the land, the equipment and everything the land produces.
- The state tells each collective farm what to farm and sets it a production target.
- All collective farm workers are organised into brigades; work set hours.
- Collective farms are allocated tractors and combine harvesters from Machine and Tractor Stations (MTS). The MTS were also used by the government to spy on the peasants.
- A collective farm is set a quota of produce it is allowed to keep in order to feed its workers.

Background and key points of collectivisation

- The Bolsheviks had given peasants land and encouraged them to move to *sovkozy* (large state collective farms) and *kolkhozy* (collective farms run by peasant committees). However, very few peasants made the move – they preferred their way.
- Stalin needed to increase food production and increase the amount of food getting to the cities. Peasant farming used inefficient methods, so needed to be mechanised.
- Peasant farming was not communist as some peasants became rich from farming (*kulaks*).
- Collectivisation started in 1928 and forced peasants into collective farms.

War on the *kulaks*

When peasants resisted collectivisation, Stalin used force. He said only *kulaks* – rich peasants – would object to collectivisation, which meant they were capitalists. Stalin ordered all *kulaks* to be purged.

Who was classed as a *kulak*? Anyone who resisted collectivisation in any way. Around 600 000 farms were 'dekulakised'.

Collectivisation

 Failures:
Peasants wrecked their equipment and killed their livestock, rather than give it up. At the same time, the government continued requisitioning grain, even when little was left. This resulted in famine in 1932–33 and millions of people died.

 Successes:
Around 90% of farmland was collectivised by 1935. Crop production did increase and bread rationing ended in 1934.

Now try this

List **three** reasons why Stalin enforced collectivisation from 1928.

Industrialisation

Stalin's plans for socialism in one country, and fears of capitalist invasion, demanded that the Soviet Union become a strong, industrial country with extraordinary speed.

Gosplan and the Five-Year Plans

In the USSR, the state decided everything.

- Gosplan (State Planning Committee) set up Five-Year Plans for industry.
- These set targets for regions to set up factories, train workers and produce set amounts of things.

1 The First Five-Year Plan, 1928–32, set iron, steel, coal, oil and electricity targets. Propaganda claimed that the targets were met a year early (not true).

2 The Second Five-Year Plan, 1933–37, for the same industries plus railways, tractors and combine harvesters.

3 The Third Five-Year Plan, 1938–41, included consumer items, e.g. radios.

Increases in production

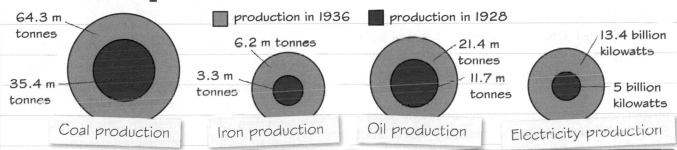

production in 1936 ■ production in 1928

64.3 m tonnes
35.4 m tonnes
Coal production

6.2 m tonnes
3.3 m tonnes
Iron production

21.4 m tonnes
11.7 m tonnes
Oil production

13.4 billion kilowatts
5 billion kilowatts
Electricity production

How was this possible?

- A massive propaganda effort made everyone work hard for the plans. Workers following the example of coal miner Alexei Stakhanov tried to exceed their targets.
- State childcare meant that women could work full time.
- Ferocious discipline forced people to work hard.
- Industry started from a low level.

Key achievements

The USSR was industrialised.

The USSR was greatly strengthened (and was able to repel the German invasion of 1941).

New towns and cities built, such as Magnitogorsk.

Unemployment dropped.

Huge new factories created from scratch to meet needs.

Improved standards of living for many people.

Massive organisational and planning problems overcome.

Problems

- 👎 Some production depended on slave labour from gulags.
- 👎 Factory conditions were often dangerous – rushing caused accidents.
- 👎 Did not improve living conditions (some lived in tents for years).
- 👎 Targets meant quality was compromised (many products broke easily).
- 👎 Targets were set low or missed targets were overlooked.
- 👎 Lots of inefficiency as one factory waited for parts from another.

Now try this

Describe the key features of industrialisation under Stalin.

Life in the Soviet Union

By 1940, living conditions in the Soviet Union had changed greatly for most people. Under Tsarism, the majority of people had been very poor. After the economic and social changes of 1928–39, living conditions were much better. But some people still had better lives than others.

Working conditions

Workers had holidays and days off, housing, health care and free education for their children, but the state had banned trade unions and workers were not allowed to change jobs. However, industrialisation had created more jobs than there were workers so there was no unemployment.

Living conditions

Housing conditions were basic but much better than what most people had before 1928. Once people had the basics, the main thing was space; most families lived squashed into one or two rooms. Conditions on the collective farms were hard and life tougher than in cities.

Women in the Soviet Union

Under Tsarism, women had very few rights. In the Soviet Union, women had equal votes to men, were paid the same, had the same educational opportunities, and it was easy to get a divorce.

Industrialisation had created so many jobs that the state needed women to work, so the state offered free childcare and equal pay.

In 1928 there were 3 million women working; by 1940 there were 13 million women working. However, men still held all the important jobs and Stalin was a big fan of family, so in 1936 divorce and abortion were made much more difficult to obtain.

Ethnic minorities in the Soviet Union

- The 15 republics of the Soviet Union were all supposed to have equal rights.
- Under Tsarism there had been a policy called Russification. The different countries of the Russian Empire had Russian as their official language.
- When the most resistance to collectivisation came from non-Russian regions, Russification came back in again.
- Stalin also targeted some nationalities in the purges.

Privilege and the party

- The Soviet Union was supposed to be a workers' state, but Communist Party members got better treatment than anyone else.
- Party members had better housing, better jobs and special perks like holidays and access to leisure clubs.
- However, under Stalin's rule no one was free as everyone lived in fear of being reported or arrested.

Now try this

Study the propaganda poster on this page. How does it portray life in the Soviet Union? Do you think it is an accurate picture of what Soviet life was like?

The words on this poster read 'Day after day, life becomes even happier'.

С КАЖДЫМ ДНЕМ ВСЕ РАДОСТНЕЕ ЖИТЬ!

The USA after the First World War

The US economy boomed during the First World War because it both lent money to, and sold its exports to Europe. The US government stepped back to let the economy manage itself, while its international policies grew more isolationist.

Impact of the war:
- Huge demand in Europe for US products.
- Huge demand in Europe for US grain.
- New export markets now open to USA.
- Europe depending on USA for loans.

Factors for growth in the USA

Government policies:
- *Laissez faire* – very pro-business.
- Tariffs – boosted US home sales.

Innovation:
- New industries (e.g. radios, fridges).
- New technology and processes – e.g. mass production.

The isolationism of the USA

The USA did not want to get dragged into any more European wars. It refused to join the League of Nations. America's view was that it should look after itself.

The USA set up 'walls' to protect its businesses from foreign competition.

 May 1921: Emergency Tariff Act
- These tariff 'walls' meant imports from outside the USA cost more than home-produced goods.

 September 1922: Fordney and McCumber Tariff Act
- American people bought US goods instead.
- In response, foreign countries put tariffs on US exports.
- As a result, the USA sold less abroad.

Laissez faire principles
- ✗ Don't weigh business down with laws.
- ✗ Don't tell business how much to pay people.
- ✓ Let business decide how to treat workers.
- ✓ Let business decide what prices to charge.

Laissez faire – French for 'leave it alone'.

Immigration restrictions
- In 1921, the Emergency Quota Act worked out how many people from each country were already in the USA, then allowed only 3% of that number in from that country as new immigrants.
- Many in the USA were prejudiced against Italians and Eastern Europeans. This was also an isolationist stance – why should the USA have to solve all Europe's problems?

Now try this

1 Explain why the Tariff Acts of 1921 and 1922 led to a decline in US exports.

2 If a government had *laissez faire* policies, would it tell a company that paid very low wages to improve wages or would the government argue that wages were none of its business?

Problem areas

Not all parts of the US economy enjoyed boom times in the 1920s. Some older industries and agriculture had difficult times. Here are some examples:

Older industries

Coal mining, shipbuilding, cotton textile manufacturers and railways didn't experience a boom.

Not consumer products.

Couldn't use mass production.

Huge demand in war for new ships, but then demand slumped after war.

Why did older industries struggle?

People switched to electricity – less coal.

People bought cars – less rail travel.

Less demand for cotton-based clothes from traditional textile producers.

Borrowing

There was over-confidence that the boom would continue. Banks kept on lending money (credit) to people who already owed more money than they could repay: there was a lack of credit control. People used this credit to buy stock market shares, expecting to be able to sell them again at a higher price as the economy kept booming.

Farming

Farming experienced a boom during the war and then immediately after it – Europe was desperate for food. So what went wrong?

US farmers took out loans to expand production – bigger farms, more machinery

⬇

But then European farming recovered – demand for US food declined

⬇

Other countries started to increase their exports too: e.g. Russia and Canada

⬇

Prohibition in USA reduced demand for barley and grapes (used to make beer and wine)

⬇

Demand for cotton fell as new materials developed for making clothes (e.g. nylon)

⬇

US farming's **overproduction** meant that farm prices fell

Poverty in the 1920s

The USA in the 1920s was an unequal society. A small number of people were very rich and a lot of people remained very poor. The Brookings Survey of 1929 found that many Americans were living in poverty.

The government could have acted to improve things. For example, it could have bought up extra production to protect farmers' incomes or stepped in to protect workers' wages from being cut. However, *laissez faire* policy said that the government should let things sort themselves out.

- Farming problems led to a lot of rural poverty. Farming wages fell in the 1920s.
- South vs. North – a lot of the big industries were in the northern states; wages were often lower in the South.
- Black vs. white – black Americans often had the lowest paid work.

Despite these problems, skilled and semi-skilled workers and women saw wages increase a lot in the 1920s.

Now try this

Explain why US farming was damaged by the invention of synthetic materials that replaced cotton for making clothes.

The US economic boom

The boom was the result of lots of different factors coming together: the huge demand around the world for US products, mass production, new developments in advertising and the stock market.

Consumerism

New ways of selling fuelled a massive consumer boom in USA – especially for new industries making consumer goods, such as radios, vacuum cleaners and pop-up toasters.

1 Advertising made people buy things they didn't know they needed.

2 Higher wages and more leisure time meant people could buy more things.

3 Hire purchase made it possible to buy expensive products in instalments.

Mass production

Mass production was an important cause of the economic boom and was pioneered by the Ford motor company.

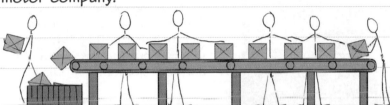

1 Mass production divided up the production process...

2 ... so each worker took only one step in the production process...

3 ... using standard parts.

4 This is called an assembly line.

The consumer boom

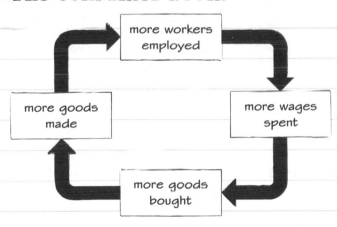

more workers employed → more wages spent → more goods bought → more goods made →

The stock market boom

People could buy shares in successful businesses

⇓

If businesses got more successful, shares would be worth more

⇓

So people bought shares hoping to sell them again to make money

⇓

The USA was growing so fast that most businesses were worth more each year

⇓

People borrowed money to spend on shares as they were so profitable: what could go wrong?

Consequences

1 People no longer ashamed to be in debt.

2 Businesses doing so well – *laissez faire* government must be best.

3 Americans wanted to keep economic success for themselves – isolationism.

4 Millions invested their money in shares.

Now try this

1   Identify **three** important causes of the economic boom in the USA.

2   Explain how mass production made products cheaper for consumers.

The roaring 20s

In the 1920s people had more money to spend and more leisure time. The brand new movie industry created a whole new form of entertainment and people couldn't get enough of glamour, excitement and celebrity.

Social impacts of the roaring 20s

Less respect for authority: Prohibition (see page 51 for more information) meant many Americans ended up breaking the law because they wanted to drink alcohol. This added to the feeling of freedom and wildness.

A sense of relief: Americans had survived the First World War, the deadly global flu epidemic that followed it, and a brief recession in the USA (1920–21) – now it was time to have fun!

America on top: After a long time trailing behind Britain, America was definitely top nation: the richest, most exciting, most powerful and most dynamic country in the world.

Literature and art: The 1920s was an amazing period for US art and literature, which added to the sense of a special time to be an American.

More money: Most people could afford to spend some money on small luxuries, often for the first time ever.

Music: The jazz music of black musicians became a craze across the nation: wild, free, uninhibited – more conservative Americans hated it.

Glamour and excitement: Hollywood movies were all about glamour and excitement. They featured new fashions and the dream of a celebrity lifestyle.

Women: Women were freer in 1920s America – they had more time, fewer restrictions and more money to spend. 'Flappers' (young women who did what they wanted without depending on men) shocked many but also, over time, helped change attitudes to women in the USA and other western countries.

The Dolly Sisters

Women

Women had taken up men's jobs and helped to win the war. It was impossible to turn back the clock completely after the men came back from the war – and most people didn't want to. More women worked and got paid better than before, housework was less time-consuming (fridges, vacuum cleaners, washing machines), businesses targeted women for products and advertised a freer, more glamorous lifestyle.

Reaction to the roaring 20s

Most Americans did not go wild and crazy in the roaring 20s. For some Americans the changes were frightening and decadent. In 1930 the Hays Code aimed to stop movies showing anything that would 'lower morals'.

Now try this

1   How did women's lives change in 1920s America?
2   How was the development of advertising and consumerism (see page 49) linked to changes for women in the 1920s?

Prohibition and gangsters

Prohibition was supposed to reduce crime and improve American morals. Instead, it increased organised crime and saw millions of Americans break the law.

What was Prohibition?

Making alcohol, transporting alcohol and selling alcohol all became illegal. Prohibition started in January 1920 and ended in December 1933. It was made law by the 18th Amendment to the Constitution.

Why was it brought in?

A lot of influential Church groups said alcohol made people behave badly. Rural America thought new immigrants in cities were dangerous drunks. Some American states had been 'dry' for years already.

What was the impact?

Gangsters found that selling alcohol was very profitable, so their numbers increased.

Corruption increased, as courts and the police were bribed.

Speakeasies were established. These were places where people could go to buy illegal alcohol.

Health risks of alcohol increased as 'moonshine' alcohol could be poisonous.

Disrespect for law increased, as many Americans wanted to drink so they broke the Prohibition law.

Organised crime

Different factors led to growth in gangster crime but Prohibition was the most important:

Prohibition

Illegal activities
- making alcohol
- smuggling alcohol
- selling alcohol

$$$

- gang wars to protect profits
- plenty of money to bribe police and courts
- reduced respect for the law
- gangs occupied whole areas and forced businesses to pay 'protection' money

The gangster Al Capone made $105 million from organised crime in 1927 – $60 million of it came from speakeasies!

Now try this

Other factors that influenced the growth of organised crime included the return of soldiers from the First World War. Why do you think that was a factor?

Racism and intolerance

Although America called itself the land of the free, racism went deep. Segregation in the South gave racism legal backing, and the courts also backed intolerance towards immigrants.

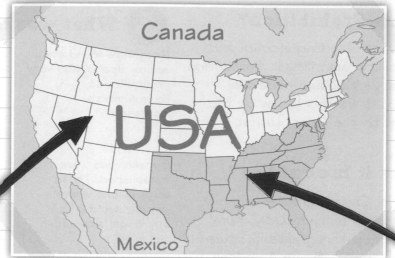

Racism in the northern states

- Many southern black Americans moved north for jobs.
- Here there was no segregation but plenty of discrimination.
- Black people usually had low-paid jobs or were unemployed.
- Black people lived in poor areas, and white and black people didn't really mix.

Racism in the southern states

- The 'Jim Crow' laws enforced segregation – separate schools and facilities.
- There were worse facilities, worse jobs and worse pay for black people.
- Black people could vote by law, but were often stopped by force or tricks.
- The Ku Klux Klan wanted a white-only America. It beat up black people and even murdered some.
- Lynchings were common in many states, including Mississippi and Alabama.

1 The Sacco and Vanzetti case of intolerance

Sacco and Vanzetti were Italian immigrants. Police thought them guilty of murder and robbery in April 1920, because they were carrying guns when arrested. Vanzetti had committed armed robbery in the past and eyewitnesses said they did it. But more eyewitnesses said they had been somewhere else. However, the judge made it clear he wanted them found guilty. There was popular protest about intolerance, but Sacco and Vanzetti were executed in 1927.

2 Scopes 'Monkey Trial'

In 1925, the state of Tennessee banned the teaching of evolution or anything but the Bible's account of creation. Biology teacher John Scopes deliberately taught evolution to test the law. Evolution theory includes the idea of humans being descended from monkeys. There was a massive media interest in the trial, and the judge decided the state law had been broken, so Scopes was found guilty and fined $100.

Now try this

Explain how the Scopes 'Monkey Trial' shows that some people's religious views caused intolerance.

The Wall Street Crash

The Wall Street Crash exposed all sorts of problems with the US economy. When the stock market crash was over, these problems still remained for everyone to see.

Weaknesses in the economy

Before the crash, there were already problems in the US economy:

Overconfidence – belief that the boom would never stop.

Almost anyone could get a loan – not enough credit control.

Big businesses kept wages low.

Too many people using loans to buy shares.

US economy

No real control on business.

Mechanisation replacing workers.

Unemployment rising.

Inequality: some people very rich, most not.

Overproduction in farming and in business.

Tariffs abroad reducing US exports.

The Wall Street Crash

Timeline

1929

Sept/Oct
People expected share prices to bounce up again, but they didn't

Sept
A few investors looked at US problems and started selling shares

Thurs 24 Oct
Panic selling of shares meant that shares were offloaded at any price

Fri 25 Oct
An attempt to stop panic by big buy-up of shares ($250 m) by group of bankers slowed panic a bit

Mon 28 Oct
More panic selling

Tues 29 Oct
Even worse: the group that bought $250 m of shares now tried to sell them too

Wed 30 Oct
Panic selling stops

Impacts of the crash

5000 banks went bankrupt and people lost their money.

Banks needed money so they called in loans.

US businesses had to pay back loans and couldn't get credit. The economy went into depression.

European countries relied on these US loans, so the export markets collapsed. World trade fell by 66%.

Businesses had to reduce production or shut down and lay off workers, which meant large job loses.

People lost their savings and couldn't afford their mortgages or hire purchase repayments, so they lost their homes and possessions. Many lost their jobs as the businesses they worked for went under.

Now try this

Write your own definitions for these key terms: **bankruptcy, investor, shares, credit, loans.**

Hoover's reaction

President Herbert Hoover and the Republicans talked about the 'rugged individualism' of ordinary Americans and the idea that 'prosperity was just around the corner'.

Hoover's approach

1 Before he became president, Hoover had organised food supplies in the First World War and food relief for Europe after the war.

2 He believed that the people suffering in the Depression should be helped too.

3 But he wanted this help to come from voluntary groups, not from the government.

Criticisms of Hoover

When people lost their jobs and their homes they would often put up a shack somewhere to live in. These shantytowns were nicknamed 'Hoovervilles', because people thought Hoover had not done enough to help.

Thousands of veterans of the First World War were campaigning for early payment of a bonus for fighting the war. In May 1932, 15 000 'Bonus Marchers' marched to Washington D.C. in protest and set up a Hooverville. Troops drove them away in July 1932.

Hoover takes action

Policy	Date	What did it do?	Effect of policy
Federal Farm Board	July 1929	Bought up surplus grain and cotton to help push farm prices up.	Spent $500m by 1932 and was then disbanded. Poor people thought this only helped the rich farmers.
Tax cuts	1930	Cut taxes with the idea that people would have more money to spend.	This meant the government started to run out of money too. In 1932 the Revenue Act put taxes up again.
Smoot–Hawley tariff	June 1930	Made imports more expensive so Americans would buy US products.	US businesses resented the tariff for making things harder. Caused a drop in imports but also exports – made things worse.
President's Organisation for Unemployment Relief (POUR)	1931	Encouraged volunteer groups and initiatives to help people and businesses.	Voluntary groups and schemes were not nearly enough to combat unemployment and poverty on this scale.
NCC – National Credit Corporation	1931	Secure private banks lent money to help restore less secure businesses and banks.	Because this meant healthy banks were being asked to lend money to less healthy banks and businesses, very little money ever got lent.
RFC – Reconstruction Finance Corporation	January 1932	A government-controlled version of NCC which made sure loans were actually paid out.	The Reconstruction Finance Corporation did lend out billions to help banks and businesses but many people thought it only helped the rich.
Emergency Relief and Construction Act	July 1932	A fund of up to $1.5 billion to help states with relief of unemployment.	Brought in as unemployment continued to rise. States had to declare they had run out of money to help the unemployed; they then got funding for public projects to generate jobs.
Federal Home Loan Bank Act	July 1932	To help local banks the government loaned to people so they could keep their homes or buy homes.	The number of people having to leave their homes because they couldn't pay their mortgages did drop, but by this time most of the damage was already done.

Now try this

President Hoover thought that if the government did things for people, they would stop trying to improve their lives and just wait for government help. Use this belief to help explain one of his policies.

The impact of the Depression

For people who lost their jobs, the Depression was a terrible time and a huge shock to everyone who had got used to the USA being the richest country in the world.

The unemployed
- Until 1932, there was very little government help for the unemployed.
- In the Depression, thousands of people were unemployed and looking for help.
- Volunteer charities could not cope with the numbers.
- After 1932, government relief agencies also struggled to cope. They introduced harsh methods to find out who the poorest were to help them first.
- But this was humiliating for people looking for help: answering questions, being inspected.
- People scavenged for food on garbage heaps, families split up to look for work. They were very desperate times.
- Many families migrated westwards for work. These included people from Oklahoma ('Okhies') and Texas ('Texies') escaping the Dust Bowl.

The homeless
- Unemployed people and families moved to the big cities from smaller towns and the countryside.
- But there was no work and nowhere for all the new people to live.
- Some travelled around the country, looking for work – migrant workers.
- Many set up shanty towns on the outskirts of cities – 'Hoovervilles'.

Impact in the countryside
- ⊗ Bank foreclosures meant families lost their farms.
- ⊗ Overproduction meant prices for farm products fell.
- ⊗ Less demand for farm products also meant falling prices.
- ⊗ Families left rural areas to look for work.

The Bonus Marchers were army veterans hit by the Depression, who set up a 'Hooverville' in Washington and campaigned for payment of a promised bonus. The Senate refused payment, despite public sympathy for the marchers. 5000 accepted loans to return home, the rest stayed till July 1932.

Resentment against Hoover

| Tax cuts looked like they just helped the rich | → | RFC help looked like it was only going to rich businesses | → | Voluntary charities felt they were failing – needed government help | → | Bonus Marchers – use of troops to clear protestors upset many people | → | The unemployed wanted work from the government |

Now try this

Hoover lost heavily to Roosevelt in the 1932 election. What are your **three** top reasons for his election defeat?

The New Deal

Roosevelt took a different approach to Hoover: federal government spent billions trying to get the USA out of depression.

Roosevelt's aims

provide relief for those in need

get people working again

rebuild confidence in banks and in shares

Roosevelt's actions

There's a lot to learn about Roosevelt's policies and lots of letters to remember. Get these two key terms straight to begin with.

 The Hundred Days: a period in 1933 when the USA passed a lot of emergency laws.

 The Alphabet Agencies: agencies set up to tackle particular problems.

Roosevelt's actions

Policy	Date	What did it do?	Effect of policy
Emergency Banking Act	March 1933	Only allowed 'safe' banks to operate, to rebuild confidence.	5000 banks reopened and people were happy to save money with them.
Reforestation Relief Act	March 1933	Set up the Civilian Conservation Corps (CCC) – created work for unemployed young men.	Critics said this wasn't real work but millions of men had volunteered by 1941. Hugely popular with the US public.
Agricultural Adjustment Act	May 1933	AAA paid farmers not to produce certain crops and products.	Tackled farm overproduction. Most farmers accepted the deal. Prices rose and farming gained confidence. But, it helped rich farmers more than poor ones.
Federal Emergency Relief Administration Act	May 1933	FERA set up the Civil Works Administration (CWA), which organised public projects such as road building to get the unemployed working.	The CWA and FERA projects created work for 20 million people. It would have been cheaper to just pay unemployment benefit but work built confidence too.
Tennessee Valley Authority Act	May 1933	TVA projects re-engineered this poor farming region which was a Dust Bowl area hit really hard by the Depression.	TVA aimed to modernise farming and provide power from dams. Meant relocating thousands of families but huge improvement in farming and loads of jobs created by the new infrastructure projects.
National Industrial Relief Act	June 1933	Set up the National Recovery Administration (NRA) to reform industry, led to better working conditions and less cut-throat competition.	NRA increased bureaucracy and made production more expensive. But the public supported it and by the time it finished (May 1935) industrial production was higher than in May 1933.

These are just some of the Hundred Days emergency laws and 'Alphabet Agencies'. You must be able to use them as examples of New Deal policies.

Now try this

What did these Alphabet Agency names stand for?

(a) AAA **(b)** NRA **(c)** FERA **(d)** CCC

Opposition and the Second New Deal

The New Deal might have been popular with voters, but there was plenty of opposition. However, the Second New Deal took the New Deal even further.

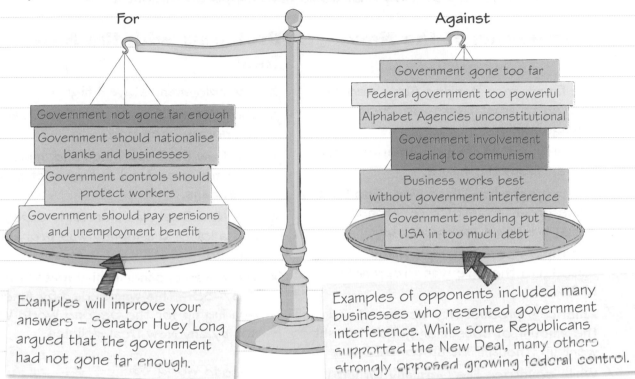

For

Government not gone far enough

Government should nationalise banks and businesses

Government controls should protect workers

Government should pay pensions and unemployment benefit

Against

Government gone too far

Federal government too powerful

Alphabet Agencies unconstitutional

Government involvement leading to communism

Business works best without government interference

Government spending put USA in too much debt

Examples will improve your answers – Senator Huey Long argued that the government had not gone far enough.

Examples of opponents included many businesses who resented government interference. While some Republicans supported the New Deal, many others strongly opposed growing federal control.

Roosevelt and the Supreme Court

- In 1935 the Supreme Court ruled some New Deal acts and agencies were unconstitutional and against the law, e.g. NRA, AAA.

- The Supreme Court was mostly anti-Roosevelt, Republican judges, who were also mostly old men.

- Roosevelt wanted more Supreme Court judges on his side and attempted to 'pack' the Supreme Court with his own supporters. This was defeated in Congress, but as judges retired or died, he replaced them with his supporters.

The Second New Deal

This began in 1935 and aimed to take government involvement further.

1 Social Security Act (1935) – old age pensions and unemployment benefit.

2 Wagner Act (1935) – replaced NRA. Employees were allowed to join a trade union if they wanted to.

3 Works Progress Administration (WPA) (1935) – funded more work programmes.

4 Resettlement Act (May 1935) – built housing for the homeless in towns and the countryside.

Now try this

1 Explain what critics meant when they complained that some of the Alphabet Agencies were unconstitutional.

2 Explain how each of the following is connected to opposition to the New Deal: Father Coughlin; the 'sick chicken case'.

Was the New Deal a success?

The extent to which the New Deal helped the USA recover from the Depression is a tricky topic because it is hard to know what would have happened without it.

Achievements of the New Deal

- ✓ The Emergency Banking Act – people started to trust banks with their savings again.
- ✓ Rebuilding confidence – Americans felt better about the future.
- ✓ The projects to create work also built some great infrastructure – roads, dams, hospitals, schools, etc.
- ✓ The rapid rise of unemployment was halted and the rate was dropping by 1935.
- ✓ America's productivity increased and the amount of consumer goods bought went up, though not up to 1928 levels.
- ✓ While countries like Germany turned to fascism following the Depression, the USA stayed a democracy.

Problems with the New Deal

- ✗ Unemployment stayed high.
- ✗ The jobs created by the New Deal were temporary ones only.
- ✗ The New Deal saw black and immigrant workers forced out in favour of white Americans.
- ✗ The New Deal was incredibly expensive and a lot of the money was probably wasted.
- ✗ There was another mini-depression in 1937–38 – this was ended by America gearing up for the Second World War, not by any New Deal policies.

The Second World War

The USA entered the war in December 1941, but supplied the Allies with food and weapons from September 1939. Lend-Lease (March 1941) provided even more help, creating many more jobs in the USA.

Assessing historical arguments

> Roosevelt's New Deal policies were mostly just extensions to Hoover's policies.

What do you think of this argument? What facts would support it or undermine it?

> The New Deal didn't get America out of the Depression, it just made things less bad than they otherwise would have been.

What do you think of this argument? What facts would support it or undermine it?

Now try this

Explain how the Second World War helped America's recovery from the Depression.

Six question types

In the Unit 2 exam you will answer six questions. Question 1 has four parts to it: (a), (b), (c) and (d), and you need to answer them all. For question 2 there is a choice between 2(a) **or** 2(b) – don't answer both of them! And for question 3 there is a choice between 3(a) **or** 3(b) – don't answer both of them either!

Question 1a

Question 1a is an inference question about a source. Inference questions ask you what you can learn from the source. For example:

> What can you learn from Source A about…

- This question is worth 4 marks.
- Link what the source says to the question.
- Explain the link you made.
- Don't just repeat what the source says.

Question 1b

Question 1b will ask you to describe a feature or characteristic of the period. For example:

> Describe the economic problems Germany experienced in the years 1919–22.

- This question is worth 6 marks.
- If you just make simple statements, the most you can get is 3 marks.
- Develop your statements with factual detail to access the higher marks.

Question 1c

Question 1c asks you to explain consequences – the impact something had on something else. For example:

> Explain the effects of the Depression on people's lives in the USA, 1929–33.

- 8 marks available.
- Support your explanation with your own knowledge.
- Make links between factors.

Question 1d

Question 1d is about causation – explaining why something happened. For example:

> Explain why Stalin was able to defeat his rivals in the struggle for power, 1924–39.

- 8 marks available.
- Say why the cause you've identified led to the outcome in the question.
- Use two or more causes.
- Prioritise which cause was most important.

Question 2

Question 2 asks you to explain change over time. For example:

> Explain how Nazi policies towards women changed in the years 1933–39.

- 8 marks available.
- Explain two or more changes.
- Prioritise the change you think is most important, or show links between changes.
- Only answer 2(a) **or** 2(b) – not both.

Question 3

Question 3 is an extended writing question. It asks you to consider causation. You will use your analysis skills in this question, weighing up which factors were the most important.

- 16 marks available, 4 are for SPaG.
- You need three consequences and you should compare how important they all were.
- The question gives you some suggested factors to use in your answer – to access the highest grades you need to use factor(s) from your own knowledge.
- Only answer 3(a) **or** 3(b) – not both.

Britain c1903-28
What skills do I need?

Unit 3 of your History GCSE is very different from Units 1 and 2. Unit 3 is about how sources are used in history. This section helps you revise the skills you need.

Your Unit 3 exam

- The exam paper has a collection of sources – between six and eight of them.
- The sources can be images or text.
- The sources will all relate to a topic you have studied.
- You answer five questions.
- Each question tests a particular skill.
- The order of the questions is always the same.

The five key skills

There are five skills, one for each of the five questions.

1. Making **inferences** from sources.
2. Considering the **purpose** of a source.
3. Explaining **causation** using a source and your own understanding.
4. Evaluating the **reliability** of sources.
5. Evaluating a **hypothesis**.

Using your own knowledge

Unit 3 isn't about remembering facts: it's about interpreting information. You use what you know about a topic to help you interpret the sources.

You need to know about the roles of women in wartime to understand this source.

The women are making explosives. This is an example of the unfamiliar jobs women did during the war.

What information does the caption give?

Photo is carefully posed, so may have been for propaganda purposes.

A photograph from the First World War showing women putting together a mine.

Now try this

What definitions would you give for each of these key terms for Unit 3?
- Inferences
- Purpose of a source
- Reliability
- Causation
- Hypothesis
- Evaluating

Five question types

The best way of seeing how these Unit 3 skills are used is to look at an old exam paper for your Unit 3 option. The questions always test the same skills in the same order.

Question 1: Inference

Inference questions will ask things like:

> What can you learn from Source A about…

- Link what the source says to the question.
- Explain the link you made.
- **Don't** just repeat what the source says.

Question 2: Purpose

Imagine one source was a poster. A purpose question will ask things like:

> What is the purpose of this poster?

- What message is the source giving?
- Think about **why** the source was created.
- Is the source pushing one point of view?

Question 3: Explaining causation

Explaining causation is about explaining why. The question will ask you to use the source and you own knowledge.

> Use Source C and your own knowledge to explain why…

Be precise with your own knowledge, giving as much useful detail as you can.

Question 4: Reliability

Reliability is about whether you can believe the source. You will need to evaluate two sources, using both the sources and your own knowledge.

> How reliable are Sources A and C as evidence...

- Reliability – think about who created the source, their intentions, how much you can trust what they say.
- Remember to evaluate using both sources and your own knowledge.

Question 5: Evaluating a hypothesis

This question asks how far you agree with a statement. You will be expected to use three sources, or more, in the exam paper and your own knowledge to decide this.

- Read the statement really carefully.
- Make a judgement about how far you agree.
- Use details from the sources to support your answer.
- Remember that there are up to three additional marks for SPaG for your answer to this question.

Now try this

What types of question are these?

(a) What can you learn from Source A about the causes of the General Strike?

(b) Source C suggests that war work helped women get the vote. How far do you agree with this interpretation?

Skills in practice

Each of the questions is worth a different number of marks. The mark scheme for each of the five question types tells you which skills you need to practice for each question.

Question 1 is worth 6 marks.
- Make two inferences.
- Support each inference.

Supporting your inference means backing up the point you make. A good way to do this is by quoting something from the source.

Question 2 is worth 8 marks.
- Identify what the representation shows or says.
- Explain how the source gives this message using **content** and **context**.
- Explain **purpose** – why it gives this message, or what is it trying to get people to do or to think?

Make sure every point you make is supported by evidence from the source or from your own knowledge.

Question 3 is worth 10 marks.
- Use one source and your own knowledge to make an explanation.
- The best answers use the source and own knowledge to explain **two** factors.

You must be precise and relevant with your knowledge.

Question 4 is worth 10 marks.
- Make a judgement on the **reliability** of the content of both sources.
- Also make a judgement about the type of sources they both are, who produced them and why – nature, origin, purpose.

There is a maximum of 8 marks for answers that do not use own knowledge – however good they are.

Question 5 is worth 16 marks.
- Link the **interpretation** to relevant details from the sources or your own knowledge.
- Use the details to show which sources support the interpretation and which challenge it.
- Review alternative views to arrive at a balanced judgement.

You cannot access Level 3 if you do not use the sources and you cannot access Level 4 if you do not use your own knowledge.

Timing

- You get 1 hour and 15 minutes.
- Question 5 carries the most marks so make sure you leave 24 minutes for answering it.
- That leaves about 10 minutes for question 1, 9 minutes for question 2, 2 minutes for question 3 and 12 minutes for question 4.

Now try this

1   Explain in your own words what the content of a source means.
2   Explain in your own words what context means when answering source questions.

Nature, origin and purpose

Working with sources involves a range of different skills. To write really good answers it helps to know about nature, origins and purpose.

Nature	Origins	Purpose
What type of source is it? (E.g. is it a diary entry, a letter, a photo, a cartoon...?)	When was the source produced and who produced it?	Why was the source produced? What is it for? Is it giving a particular message?

Working with sources

Think about nature, origins and purpose when you are inferring from sources, making judgements about reliability or purpose, or making evaluations about hypotheses.

Content – Shows a woman being restrained in a prison cell while being force-fed through a tube in her nose. 'Votes for women' is written on the cell wall.

Origins – Designed in 1914 for the WSPU, so the source was created for the suffragettes.

Purpose – To shock people about the government's actions (note the use of the word 'torture') and convince them to support the suffragette cause. You can say a lot about reliability and usefulness from thinking through the purpose.

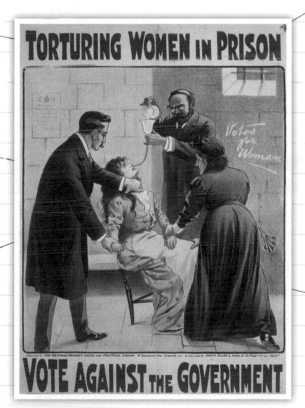

Source A: A WPSU poster from 1914.

Context – Women hunger strikers being force fed in prison and the 'Votes for women' message on the wall means this is about suffragettes. Make careful note of details in the source and use them to support the answer you give.

Nature – This is a political poster. Election posters are not reliable representations of fact but they are very useful to historians as evidence of what political groups were trying to achieve.

Now try this

Look at the source on page 60. Write a sentence about the source for each of these headings: Content, Context, Origins, Purpose, Nature.

Applying your skills

Have a go at applying different source skills to this source, which connects to the topic of the part played by the British on the Western Front.

Content: What information can you get from this source?

Origins: Who produced this source and when? (Check the caption for this information.)

Nature: What type of source is this? (The caption will help you here, too.)

> **Source A:** *From one of the first military histories of the First World War, published in 1917 by the well-known poet and military historian John Masefield, who had served as a hospital orderly on the Western Front in 1915.*
>
> It was the same all along the front. The fact now being painfully grasped was that artillery alone could not snuff out every machine-gun post, and yet just one machine-gun could rip a battalion to pieces. And there were scores of them in action, firing from concrete dugouts or the lips of the shell craters. Never again would they have such a target.

Context: What links can you make between this source and the issues you've studied in this topic?

Purpose: What do you think this source is trying to do? What message is it trying to give and why? (Use the caption and the language of the source to help with this.)

Here's a question 1 about this source and part of a student's answer:

Here's a question 4 about this source and part of a student's answer:

Worked example

What can you learn from Source A about the impact of 'new weapons' on the Western Front?
(6 marks)

I can learn that machine guns had a major impact because the source says that just one machine gun could rip a battalion to pieces.

Worked example

How reliable are Sources A and B [not shown] as evidence of the impact of 'new weapons' on the Western Front?
(10 marks)

Source A is reliable because it is a contemporary source (from 1917) where an eye-witness explains why the German defences were very hard to break through.

A full answer would be much longer.

Now try this

Read the **two** example answers on this page. What are they missing? How could you improve them?

Question 1 requires two supported inferences, but in question 4 you need to think about the NOP and use your own knowledge. You can also talk about the limitations of each source – what it doesn't say, or what makes it unreliable.

The Liberals and social reform

In 1903...

- Women could not vote in national elections.
- Many felt that a woman's place was in the home, not in politics.
- The right to vote had been extended to more men in 1884, and rights and opportunities for women were improving.

Campaign for women's suffrage (the vote)

NUWSS (Suffragists): used persuasion and petitions to parliament.

WFL: used peaceful protest such as not paying their taxes.

WSPU (Suffragettes): used militant protest, including chaining themselves to railings and attacking politicians and their property.

Government reaction

- Imprisoned suffragettes often went on hunger strike, so the authorities would force-feed them – this was dangerous and painful.
- The 'Cat and Mouse Act' allowed the authorities to release ill hunger strikers and re-arrest them when they were fit again.

In 1900, the government did very little to help the poorest in society. Following the 1906 election, the new Liberal government brought in major social reforms.

School Meals Act (1906)
- Schools provided free school meals.

Children's Charter (1908)
- Protection from neglect.
- No fireworks, tobacco or alcohol.
- Juvenile courts and borstals rather than adult prisons.

Helping young and old

Old Age Pensions Act (1908)
Small pensions were paid to people:
- over 70
- earning less than £31 per year.
This only helped the very poorest, but was very popular.

Medical Inspections (1907)
- Schools provided free medical inspections so illnesses could be identified and treated.

The Labour Exchange Act (1909)

- The unemployed registered at labour exchanges to find work.
- Helped employers find workers.

National Insurance Act (1911)

- Workers, employers and government contributed.
- Workers were paid 10 shillings a week sick pay when ill.
- Workers in a few trades could get 7 shillings a week unemployment benefit (dole) if out of work and could claim unemployment for up to 15 weeks.
- Not all male workers were covered and it didn't apply to women.

Now try this

Write down at least one way in which Liberal reforms helped **a)** the young; **b)** the old; **c)** workers.

The part played by the British on the Western Front

The BEF (British Expeditionary Force) was sent to France in August 1914. Here's a reminder of some key facts that will help you to understand the sources.

The BEF and 1914

- The German's **Schlieffen Plan** involved attacking France through Belgium, avoiding the heavily defended French–German border.
- But it took longer than planned to get through Belgium.
- The British Expeditionary Force (BEF) had been dispatched to help protect Belgium and France.
- The Germans were halted at the **Battle of the Marne**: the Schlieffen Plan had **failed**.

Trench warfare

- Lines of trenches defended by barbed wire and machine guns.
- Attacks were costly in men and rarely achieved a breakthrough.
- Instead both sides settled for attrition: making the enemy lose more men and equipment than you lost.

The Somme (1916) was planned as a breakthrough. Seven days of artillery bombardment was supposed to destroy German defences, but the Germans had sheltered in deep dugouts. German machine guns killed 20 000 British troops on the first day of the battle. By mid-November 1916, 420 000 British soldiers had died, and the Allies had advanced just 5 miles.

Timeline

Events of 1914

1 **Battle of Mons** (23 Aug, 1914): heavily outnumbered, the BEF fell back with the French army to the River Marne

2 **Battle of the Marne** (5–11 Sept, 1914): Germans pushed back to River Aisne

3 Germans dug **trenches** to defend themselves. British and French dug trenches, too

4 **The race for the sea:** both sides rushed north to try to break through before defences went up

5 **Ypres** (Oct–Nov 1914): Germans lost 134 000 troops trying to break through, French and British lost 142 000 troops stopping them

6 **Stalemate** on the Western Front (Dec 1914): both sides constructed heavily fortified trench defences

Poison gas – but gas masks were effective and gas could drift to your own side.

Tanks – machine-gun-proof but broke down a lot.

New weapons and methods

Creeping barrage – artillery shelled just ahead of the advancing infantry. Hard not to kill your own troops.

General Haig commanded the British at the Somme. Failure meant he was heavily criticised after his death as 'the Butcher of the Somme'.

The USA joined the war in April 1917. The Germans knew this meant defeat was likely.
- General Ludendorff launched a massive offensive in March 1918: a last gamble.
- Nearly succeeded: British troops were heavily involved in defending the Front. The Allied lines were pushed back.

- But the Germans were short on supplies and reinforcements. In June 1917 US troops started to arrive and in July 1918 the Allies counter-attacked.
- At 11 o'clock on 11 November 1918, the war ended.

Now try this

Explain why trench warfare produced stalemate between the sides.

The Home Front and social change 1914–18

The First World War meant that government became more powerful than it had been in Britain before. Here's a reminder of some key facts that will help you to understand the sources.

DORA

The government passed **DORA**, the Defence of the Realm Act (1914).

Control over key industries – focus production on war needs.

Control over people – activities that might damage the war effort were restricted.

DORA

Propaganda – encourage recruitment, boost morale.

Censorship – prevent damage to war effort and morale.

Censorship includes reading and editing letters from the Front. Propaganda includes recruitment posters.

Rationing

DORA gave the government the right to introduce **rationing**.

- Both Britain and Germany used their powerful navies to blockade ports and stop supplies getting through.

- German U-boats became very successful at sinking merchant ships.

- British farmers could not grow enough food to support the whole country.

- In 1917 food rationing was voluntary.

- By 1918 the government had to make rationing compulsory for foods like sugar, meat and butter.

- Rationing, growing more food and successful tactics against U-boats (convoy systems) meant no one starved.

Recruitment and conscription

- At first, young men were keen to sign up and 'do their bit'.

- **Pals battalions** encouraged this.

- The huge losses meant recruitment dwindled.

- The **Derby Scheme** asked men to promise to serve if asked – but less than half agreed.

- January 1916: all single men aged 18–41 could be called up.

- May 1916: married men, 18–41 called up.

Conscientious objectors refused to fight. **Tribunals** often gave them non-combatant roles. **Absolutists** refused these and were jailed. Popular opinion was strongly against 'conshies'.

Women and the war effort

- The suffragettes organised a '**Right to Serve**' demonstration in July 1915.

- The losses of men at the Front and the introduction of conscription increased the need for women to take on men's jobs.

- Now as well as office and transport jobs and working in the **Women's Land Army**, women took on jobs in heavy industry, including making armaments.

- By the end of the war, almost 800 000 women were working in engineering.

- From 1917, women could work for the Armed Forces: about 100 000 did so.

- After the war, men took the jobs back.

- But women got the vote, partly in recognition of war service.

Now try this

Give **three** reasons why conscientious objectors were so unpopular during the First World War.

Economic and social change 1918-28

The changing role of women

After the war, the political position of women improved:

- Women over 30 got the vote in 1918; extended to women over 21 in 1928.
- Women could become MPs from 1918.

However women's social and economic position did not change much:

- Women were expected to give up their jobs when the men came home.
- In 1911, 35% of all women had jobs; by 1931 this was 34%.
- Most girls left school at 14.

Industrial unrest 1918-26

- Trade union membership doubled during the war.
- When the war ended, strikes broke out again and many more workers joined trade unions.
- Heavy industries, boosted during the war, slumped after it and unemployment rose.

The Samuel Commission report (1926):

- no increase in working day
- wages should be cut
- mine owners must modernise pits.

Timeline

Unrest in mining

15 April 1921: 'Black Friday': the railwaymen and transport workers pulled out of a Triple Alliance strike to support the coalminers

31 July 1925: 'Red Friday': Prime Minister Baldwin announced a 9 month subsidy for coal mining wages

1 May 1926: miners' subsidy ran out

4 May 1926: the General Strike began: 3 million workers went on strike to support the miners

1 April 1921: coal mines returned to private ownership. Coal prices fell, and the mine owners cut wages

1925: coal prices fell again: pay cuts and longer hours. The Triple Alliance stuck together and threatened a general strike

10 March 1926: Samuel Commission report published

3 May 1926: talks between the government and the TUC broke down

The General Strike (4–12 May 1926)

Government actions:

- propaganda against strike
- took strong line: refused to negotiate
- protected food supplies
- stockpiled coal supplies
- spent £433 million combating the strike.

Effects of the strike

- TUC called off the strike because:
  - strong government response
  - fear of violence
  - lack of Labour Party support
  - shortage of funds.
- Trades Disputes and Trade Unions Act (1927) banned sympathy strikes.
- Coalminers stayed on strike with great suffering. Those that got their jobs back had lower pay and longer hours.
- Big drop in morale for unions.

Now try this

How did the government portray the General Strike, and was it a fair picture?

Britain c1931–51
What skills do I need?

Unit 3 of your History GCSE is very different from Units 1 and 2. Unit 3 is about how sources are used in history. This section helps you revise the skills you need.

Your Unit 3 exam

- The exam paper has a collection of sources – between six and eight of them.
- The sources can be images or text.
- The sources will all relate to a topic you have studied.
- You answer five questions.
- Each question tests a particular skill.
- The order of the questions is always the same.

The five key skills

There are five skills, one for each of the five questions.

1 Making **inferences** from sources.

2 Considering the **purpose** of a source.

3 Explaining **causation** using a source and your own understanding.

4 Evaluating the **reliability** of sources.

5 Evaluating a **hypothesis**.

Using your own knowledge

Unit 3 isn't about remembering facts: it's about interpreting information. You use what you know about a topic to help you interpret the sources.

You need to know about the events of the Blitz to understand this source.

Royal family inspecting bomb damage. This is an example of attempts to keep morale high.

Churchill looking determined. Why was this picture painted this way?

What information does the caption give?

A painting from 1942 showing the Blitz on London, featuring Churchill, and King George VI and Queen Elizabeth.

Now try this

What definitions would you give for each of these key terms for Unit 3?
- Inferences
- Purpose of a source
- Reliability
- Causation
- Hypothesis
- Evaluating

Five question types

The best way of seeing how these Unit 3 skills are used is to look at an old exam paper for your Unit 3 option. The questions always test the same skills in the same order.

Question 1: Inference

Inference questions will ask things like:

> What can you learn from Source A about…

- Link what the source says to the question.
- Explain the link you made.
- **Don't** just repeat what the source says.

Question 2: Purpose

Imagine one source was a poster. A purpose question will ask things like:

> What is the purpose of this poster?

- What message is the source giving?
- Think about **why** the source was created.
- Is the source pushing one point of view?

Question 3: Explaining causation

Explaining causation is about explaining why. The question will ask you to use the source and you own knowledge.

> Use Source C and your own knowledge to explain why…

> Be precise with your own knowledge, giving as much useful detail as you can.

Question 4: Reliability

Reliability is about whether you can believe the source. You will need to evaluate two sources, using both the sources and your own knowledge.

> How reliable are Sources A and C as evidence…

- Reliability – think about who created the source, their intentions, how much you can trust what they say.
- Remember to evaluate using both sources and your own knowledge.

Question 5: Evaluating a hypothesis

This question asks how far you agree with a statement. You will be expected to use three sources, or more, in the exam paper and your own knowledge to decide this.

- Read the statement really carefully.
- Make a judgement about how far you agree.
- Use details from the sources to support your answer.
- Remember that there are up to three additional marks for SPaG for your answer to this question.

Now try this

What types of question are these?

(a) What can you learn from Source A about how Britain won the Battle of Britain?

(b) Source D suggests that the NHS was a great success. How far do you agree with this interpretation?

70

Skills in practice

Each of the questions is worth a different number of marks. The mark scheme for each of the five question types tells you which skills you need to practice for each question.

Question 1 is worth 6 marks.
- Make two inferences.
- Support each inference.

Supporting your inference means backing up the point you make. A good way to do this is by quoting something from the source.

Question 2 is worth 8 marks.
- Identify what the representation shows or says.
- Explain how the source gives this message using **content** and **context**.
- Explain **purpose** – why it gives this message, or what is it trying to get people to do or to think?

Make sure every point you make is supported by evidence from the source or from your own knowledge.

Question 3 is worth 10 marks.
- Use one source and your own knowledge to make an explanation.
- The best answers use the source and own knowledge to explain **two** factors.

You must be precise and relevant with your knowledge.

Question 4 is worth 10 marks.
- Make a judgement on the **reliability** of the content of both sources.
- Also make a judgement about the type of sources they both are, who produced them and why – nature, origin, purpose.

There is a maximum of 8 marks for answers that do not use own knowledge – however good they are.

Question 5 is worth 16 marks.
- Link the **interpretation** to relevant details from the sources or your own knowledge.
- Use the details to show which sources support the interpretation and which challenge it.
- Review alternative views to arrive at a balanced judgement.

You cannot access Level 3 if you do not use the sources and you cannot access Level 4 if you do not use your own knowledge.

Timing

- You get 1 hour and 15 minutes.
- Question 5 carries the most marks so make sure you leave 24 minutes for answering it.
- That leaves about 10 minutes for question 1, 9 minutes for question 2, 2 minutes for question 3 and 12 minutes for question 4.

Now try this

1   Explain in your own words what the content of a source means.
2   Explain in your own words what context means when answering source questions.

Nature, origin and purpose

Working with sources involves a range of different skills. To write really good answers it helps to know about nature, origins and purpose.

Nature	**Origins**	**Purpose**
What type of source is it? (E.g. is it a diary entry, a letter, a photo, a cartoon...?)	When was the source produced and who produced it?	Why was the source produced? What is it for? Is it giving a particular message?

Working with sources

Think about nature, origins and purpose when you are inferring from sources, making judgements about reliability or purpose, or making evaluations about hypotheses.

Content – Shows a soldier telling a boy dressed as a soldier to leave London. The background shows rubble with a Union flag.

Nature – Government propaganda poster. Propaganda has a strong purpose and is reliable only as an indicator of what the government wanted to happen.

Origins – Designed in 1940–41 for the Ministry of Health.

Context – Produced when London was being heavily bombed and children were being evacuated to the countryside. Make careful note of details in the source and use them to support the answer you give.

Purpose – Designed to encourage families to evacuate any children not yet evacuated from London. Also to show the brave spirit of the British. You can say a lot about reliability and usefulness from thinking through the purpose.

LEAVE THIS TO US SONNY — <u>YOU</u> OUGHT TO BE OUT OF LONDON

MINISTRY OF HEALTH EVACUATION SCHEME

Source A: Government source, produced during the Blitz (Sept 1940–May 1941).

Now try this

Look at the source on page 69. Write a sentence about the source for each of these headings: Content, Context, Origin, Purpose, Nature.

Applying your skills

Have a go at applying different source skills to this source, which connects to the topic of the changing role of women.

Content: What information can you get from this source?

Context: What links can you make between this source and issues you've studied in this topic?

Source A: *From an interview with a 28-year-old married woman interviewed by Mass Observation in 1944. Mass Observation was a social research project and not part of government propaganda.*

It is far better for a woman to continue with the job for which she is suited, and to pay the right kind of person to look after her home and children, than to become a drudge herself, if housework is drudgery to her. But I think a married woman should work no more than 40 hours a week, and she should always consider her family before her job.

Origins: Who produced this source and when? (Check the caption for this information.)

Nature: What type of source is this? (The caption will help you here, too.)

Purpose: What do you think this source is trying to do? What message is it trying to give? (Use the caption and the language of the source to help with this.)

Here's a question 1 about this source and a student's answer:

Worked example

What can you learn from Source A about the changing role of women in wartime Britain?

(6 marks)

The source shows that this woman believed it was right for women to work rather than to be housewives if they wanted to; in fact she says it is 'far better for a woman to continue with her job' than be a housewife if she likes her job.

Here's a question 4 about this source and a student's answer:

Worked example

How reliable is are Sources A and B [not shown] as evidence of attitudes to women working in wartime Britain?

(10 marks)

Source A is reliable because it is a contemporary source (from 1944) recorded by Mass Observation who were not part of the government's Ministry of Information so not propaganda.

A full answer would be much longer.

Now try this

Read the **two** example answers on this page. What are they missing? How could you improve them?

Question 1 requires two supported inferences, but in question 4 you need to think about the NOP and use your own knowledge. You can also talk about the limitations of each of the two sources – what it doesn't say, or what makes it unreliable.

The impact of the Depression 1931-39

Unemployment

Unemployment in the 1930s was not the same throughout Britain:

Unemployment highest in the coal, iron and steel, cotton and shipbuilding industries.

Unemployment was highest in north and east of England and in Scotland and Wales.

New light industries did better: concentrated in England, especially the London area.

Unemployment – government responses

- The government had huge debts and made huge public spending cuts.
- It launched a publicity campaign to try to justify the cuts.
- A '**means test**' was proposed in 1931 because there wasn't enough money to pay benefits. Thousands failed the test and lost benefits.
- The **Special Areas Act** (1934) put £2 million into Scotland, Tyneside, Cumberland and South Wales.
- The **Unemployment Act** (1934) set up a board to run the '**dole**'.

Jarrow in the 1930s

- Shipyard owners set up the **NSS** (National Shipbuilders Securities Ltd) in 1930 to make shipbuilding efficient.
- The NSS closed **Palmer's shipyard**, in 1934: Jarrow's main employer.
- By 1935, unemployment in Jarrow was at 64%.

The Jarrow Crusade

The Jarrow Crusade

In 1936 people in Jarrow sent 200 workers on a march to London with a petition to ask for work. The National Unemployed Workers' Movement (NUWM), backed by the Labour Party, was also organising a national hunger march. But the people of Jarrow did not want to join this march: the NUWM was associated with communists.

Response to the Jarrow Crusade

- Popular opinion varied: the marchers got a lot of support but also criticism.
- The government did not accept the petition or act to bring jobs to Jarrow.

The experience of the unemployed

- People in depressed regions were generally hit hardest.
- Prices rose while benefits were reduced, hitting living standards hard. Many on the 'dole' were undernourished.
- The means test was demeaning – those on the 'dole' had to prove that they were poor enough.

Now try this

Explain why the people of Jarrow did not want to combine their march with the NUWM's.

Britain at war 1939-45

On 22 June 1940, France surrendered to Germany. Britain was left to fight Germany alone. Here's a reminder of some key facts that will help you understand sources for this topic.

The retreat of the BEF

- The **BEF** was forced to retreat from the German *Blitzkrieg* and evacuate from Dunkirk (May–June 1940: Operation Dynamo).
- The government asked owners of small boats to go to **Dunkirk** to help the navy evacuate the soldiers: over 338 000 troops were rescued.
- Dunkirk meant Britain still had an army to fight the Germans.

Churchill knew **morale** was essential if Britain was to survive the war – '**Dunkirk spirit**'.

Blitzkrieg!

The German invasion of the Low Countries and France used *Blitzkrieg* – a new military tactic combining planes, tanks, artillery and ground troops in a highly mobile attack.

The Battle of Britain

The Battle of Britain lasted several months. The Germans failed to win the control in the air necessary for an invasion of Britain.

- Although the *Luftwaffe* had many more planes, the RAF had more fighter planes, and a better design: the Spitfire.
- Britain also had radar, so it knew where attacks were coming from.
- Factories in Britain worked hard to build more and more Spitfires.

Key events in the Battle of Britain

10 July to 6 September, 1940: *Luftwaffe* attacks on British coast, especially RAF radar stations, and then later British airfields.

⬇

7 to 15 September: *Luftwaffe* thinks RAF is beaten and attacks London – start of the **Blitz**.

⬇

15 September: With the *Luftwaffe* defeated, Hitler calls off the invasion of Britain.

D-Day – why did it succeed?

Deceptions – very effective.

USA – huge numbers of troops and equipment.

Planning – meant good supplies.

Germany – fighting on two fronts.

The defeat of Germany

After D-Day, Germany was under pressure from all sides. The USA brought vast amounts of weaponry into the war, making German defeat almost inevitable.

Allied generals pushed towards Germany but made some major mistakes:

- Hurried plans to liberate the Netherlands saw a big defeat at Arnhem (September 1944).
- Germans counterattacked at the Battle of the Bulge (December 1944), but they lost troops they could not replace.

By April 1945, Soviet troops entered Berlin. Hitler killed himself and the Germans surrendered.

Now try this

Give **three** reasons why the Allies won the war.

The Home Front 1939–45

As the war continued, the government took an increasing role in everyday life. Here's a reminder of some key facts that will help you understand sources for this topic.

Government control – information

The Ministry of Information controlled:

- **Censorship** – making sure important information was not given away or public morale weakened by bad news.
- **Propaganda** – sending out messages to encourage the public to help the war effort. This included films, radio talks, posters and leaflets.

Government control – rationing

- Britain was dependent on food imports.
- German **U-boats** sank supply ships and rationing started in January 1940.
- As well as rationing, people were encouraged to grow their own food.
- Rations meant there was not much food and it was very monotonous.
- A black market sold food illegally.

The changing role of women

- The **Women's Land Army** helped supply Britain with the food it needed.
- In December 1941 unmarried women aged 20–30 were conscripted: they could choose between the armed services, civil defence or industry.
- After the war, it was seen as most important to give jobs back to men.
- But women were more likely to work in the 1950s than before.

Women's Land Army.

Preparing for bombing and invasion

Before the war started, the government was sure Germany would bomb cities.

- From 1 September 1939, 3 million children were **evacuated** from cities likely to be bombed. Many returned home when no bombs fell (yet!).
- Other preparations included **air-raid shelters** and the **blackout**.
- From May 1940, the **Home Guard** was trained to fight a German invasion.

The Blitz (7 September 1940–May 1941)

- London and many other cities were targeted. Civilians targeted so that the public would want to surrender.
- 43 000 civilians killed and 2 million made homeless. However public support for Churchill and the war continued.
- From 1944–45, new weapons were used: the **V1** and **V2** bombs.
- The V1s and V2s killed about 9000 people and were terrifying. But many failed to reach Britain at all.

Now try this

Give **three** ways in which the war changed women's lives in Britain.

Labour in power 1945–51

Once the Second World War had ended, the British government faced many difficult tasks. Here's a reminder of some key facts that will help you understand sources for this topic.

The reasons for Labour's election victory in 1945

- Churchill was complacent: he thought his popularity as a war leader would win him the general election of 5 July 1945.

- But Churchill's Conservative Party did not recognise how much the British people wanted reform.

- Churchill said Labour's socialist policies would never work without a 'Gestapo' to run them – a big mistake.

- Many people remembered the 1930s when the state did not seem to do enough to reduce people's suffering.

Beveridge and the attack on want

Beveridge's report was published in December 1942. It said the state should support its citizens 'from cradle to grave' and must fight '**five giants**'.

> 1 **Want** – people not having enough basic things, like food.
>
> 2 **Ignorance** – lack of good education.
>
> 3 **Disease** – people not having access to proper medical care.
>
> 4 **Squalor** – poor living conditions.
>
> 5 **Idleness** – unemployment.

Fighting 'want'

Three Acts were designed to combat 'want':

> 1945: **Family Allowances Act** – paid mothers 5 shillings per week for every child after the first one.

> 1946: **National Insurance Act** – workers and employers paid into the National Insurance Scheme, which funded unemployment, maternity and sickness benefit, and old-age pensions.

> 1948: **National Assistance Act** – National Assistance Boards set up to help those not covered by national insurance.

The NHS

The National Health Service (NHS) was designed to be **comprehensive** – for everyone and **free** at the point of use.

The National Health Service Act (1946) set up the NHS. It did not create new hospitals or new doctors or dentists – instead it made sure that everyone could use these services.

Hospitals were put into public ownership. Doctors and dentists still worked for themselves, but had a contract to provide their services to the NHS. Health services were organised for each local authority.

Opposition to the NHS

- The **BMA** (British Medical Association) wanted reform, so that those needing free health care could get it. However doctors wanted to stay independent – they did not want to be controlled by the state.

- The BMA demanded changes to the Act, so the NHS didn't start until 1948.

Using the NHS

- The government did not realise how popular the NHS would be, or how much it would cost.

- Poorer people got access to services they could never have afforded before.

- **Prescription charges** had to be introduced to meet costs in 1949 and 1951 – but not for poor people.

Now try this

Give **three** reasons why people in Britain in 1945 wanted the state to do more to help people.

Britain c1951–79 What skills do I need?

Unit 3 of your History GCSE is very different from Units 1 and 2. Unit 3 is about how sources are used in history. This section helps you revise the skills you need.

Your Unit 3 exam

- The exam paper has a collection of sources – between six and eight of them.
- The sources can be images or text.
- The sources will all relate to a topic you have studied.
- You answer five questions.
- Each question tests a particular skill.
- The order of the questions is always the same.

The five key skills

There are five skills, one for each of the five questions.

1 Making **inferences** from sources.

2 Considering the **purpose** of a source.

3 Explaining **causation** using a source and your own understanding.

4 Evaluating the **reliability** of sources.

5 Evaluating a **hypothesis**.

Using your own knowledge

Unit 3 isn't about remembering facts: it's about interpreting information. You use what you know about a topic to help you interpret the sources.

You need to know about the Winter of Discontent in 1979 to understand this source.

Huge amounts of rubbish piled up – refuse collection is not working. Strikes?

What information does the caption give?

Photo selected to show one part of the street – not possible to tell if this is one isolated rubbish heap or everywhere is covered in rubbish.

A photograph of an East London street in 1979, during the Winter of Discontent.

Now try this

What definitions would you give for each of these key terms for Unit 3?
- Inferences
- Purpose of a source
- Reliability
- Causation
- Hypothesis
- Evaluating

Five question types

The best way of seeing how these Unit 3 skills are used is to look at an old exam paper for your Unit 3 option. The questions always test the same skills in the same order.

Question 1: Inference

Inference questions will ask things like:

> What can you learn from Source A about...

- Link what the source says to the question.
- Explain the link you made.
- **Don't** just repeat what the source says.

Question 2: Purpose

Imagine one source was a poster. A purpose question will ask things like:

> What is the purpose of this poster?

- What message is the source giving?
- Think about **why** the source was created.
- Is the source pushing one point of view?

Question 3: Explaining causation

Explaining causation is about explaining why. The question will ask you to use the source and you own knowledge.

> Use Source C and your own knowledge to explain why...

> Be precise with your own knowledge, giving as much useful detail as you can.

Question 4: Reliability

Reliability is about whether you can believe the source. You will need to evaluate two sources, using both the sources and your own knowledge.

> How reliable are Sources A and C as evidence...

- Reliability – think about who created the source, their intentions, how much you can trust what they say.
- Remember to evaluate using both sources and your own knowledge.

Question 5: Evaluating a hypothesis

This question asks how far you agree with a statement. You will be expected to use three sources, or more, in the exam paper and your own knowledge to decide this.

- Read the statement really carefully.
- Make a judgement about how far you agree.
- Use details from the sources to support your answer.
- Remember that there are up to three additional marks for SPaG for your answer to this question.

Now try this

What types of question are these?

(a) What can you learn from Source A about changes in the education system in England after 1965?

(b) Source B suggests that most people in Britain were against the abolition of the death penalty. How far do you agree with this interpretation?

Skills in practice

Each of the questions is worth a different number of marks. The mark scheme for each of the five question types tells you which skills you need to practice for each question.

Question 1 is worth 6 marks.
- Make two inferences.
- Support each inference.

Supporting your inference means backing up the point you make. A good way to do this is by quoting something from the source.

Question 2 is worth 8 marks.
- Identify what the representation shows or says.
- Explain how the source gives this message using **content** and **context**.
- Explain **purpose** – why it gives this message, or what is it trying to get people to do or to think?

Make sure every point you make is supported by evidence from the source or from your own knowledge.

Question 3 is worth 10 marks.
- Use one source and your own knowledge to make an explanation.
- The best answers use the source and own knowledge to explain **two** factors.

You must be precise and relevant with your knowledge.

Question 4 is worth 10 marks.
- Make a judgement on the **reliability** of the content of both sources.
- Also make a judgement about the type of sources they both are, who produced them and why – nature, origin, purpose.

There is a maximum of 8 marks for answers that do not use own knowledge – however good they are.

Question 5 is worth 16 marks.
- Link the **interpretation** to relevant details from the sources or your own knowledge.
- Use the details to show which sources support the interpretation and which challenge it.
- Review alternative views to arrive at a balanced judgement.

You cannot access Level 3 if you do not use the sources and you cannot access Level 4 if you do not use your own knowledge.

Timing
- You get 1 hour and 15 minutes.
- Question 5 carries the most marks so make sure you leave 24 minutes for answering it.
- That leaves about 10 minutes for question 1, 9 minutes for question 2, 2 minutes for question 3 and 12 minutes for question 4.

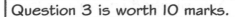

Now try this

1 Explain in your own words what the content of a source means.
2 Explain in your own words what context means when answering source questions.

Nature, origin and purpose

Working with sources involves a range of different skills. To write really good answers it helps to know about nature, origins and purpose.

Nature	Origins	Purpose
What type of source is it? (E.g. is it a diary entry, a letter, a photo, a cartoon...?)	When was the source produced and who produced it?	Why was the source produced? What is it for? Is it giving a particular message?

Working with sources

Think about nature, origins and purpose when you are inferring from sources, making judgements about usefulness or purpose, or making evaluations about hypotheses.

Content – Shows various imagined scenarios if gender roles were reversed and women acted like men and men acted like women.

Context – Women's Lib argued for equality between women and men in all aspects of life. It was controversial because many men and women in the 1970s felt that gender roles were natural to men and women and allowed society to function in an orderly way.

Nature – Political cartoon, drawn by a cartoonist to appear in a daily newspaper. The source uses funny drawings with text captions providing commentary or dialogue.

NOW THAT WOMEN'S LIB HAS DAWNED ... by Cummings

"Young woman! Will you be able to keep my son in the manner to which he's been accustomed?"

"We've run out of petrol!"

"Caught you! With your secretary on your knee!"

"Why can't I have an E-Type Jaguar like Mr. Jones next door?"

"Darling! I'm expecting a happy event!"

Purpose – Drawn to provide a humorous perspective of a very recent political event in a daily newspaper. The newspaper editor selected cartoonists and cartoons that reflected the political bias of the newspaper.

A cartoon from the *Daily Express* newspaper, 9 February 1973. The cartoon was published after the Conservative government decided to discuss an anti-discrimination bill following public pressure to end discrimination against women.

Origins – Drawn by cartoonist Cummings for the *Daily Express* newspaper 9 February 1973. Michael Cummings was a regular cartoonist for the *Express* and frequently criticised the Labour Party and 'liberal' social values.

Now try this

Look at the source on page 78. Write a sentence about the source for each of these headings: Content, Context, Origins, Purpose, Nature.

Applying your skills

Have a go at applying different source skills to this source, which connects to the topic on media, communications and leisure 1960–79.

Content: What information can you get from this source?

Origins: Who produced this source and when? (Check the caption for this information.)

Source A: *From an interview with George Harrison in the Daily Mirror in November 1966. George Harrison was the guitarist in The Beatles.*

We've had four years doing what everybody else wanted us to do. Now we are doing what we want to do. But whatever we do, it has to be real and progressive. Everything we've done so far has been rubbish... Other people might like what we've been doing, but we're not kidding ourselves. It doesn't mean a thing to what we want to do now.

Context: What links can you make between this source and issues you've studied in this topic?

Nature: What type of source is this? (The caption will help you here, too.)

Purpose: What do you think this source is trying to do? What message is it trying to give? (Use the caption and the language of the source to help with this.)

Here's a question 1 about this source and part of a student's answer:

Worked example

What can you learn from Source A about Beatlemania? **(6 marks)**

George Harrison felt Beatlemania was manufactured because he says: 'We've had four years doing what everybody else wanted us to do.'

A full answer would be much longer.

Here's a question 2 about this source and part of a student's answer:

Worked example

Use Source A and your own knowledge to explain The Beatles' huge success after 1963. **(8 marks)**

George Harrison clearly suggests that The Beatles' success up to 1966 was not due just to their own talents. The Beatles were signed to EMI, and their image was completely changed by the record company to make them more popular. So one reason for their success was definitely the way they were managed.

Now try this

Read the **two** example answers on this page. What are they missing? How could you improve them?

Question 1 requires two supported inferences. In question 2 you need to use the source and your own knowledge to explain two factors.

British society and economy in the 1950s

New economic, social, cultural and political developments followed the end of the Second World War. Here's a reminder of some key facts that will help you understand sources for this topic.

Family roles in the 1950s

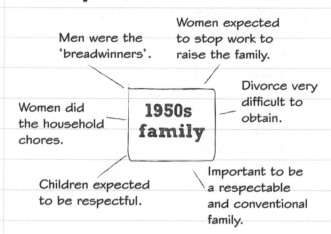

Men were the 'breadwinners'.

Women expected to stop work to raise the family.

Divorce very difficult to obtain.

Women did the household chores.

1950s family

Children expected to be respectful.

Important to be a respectable and conventional family.

Leisure activities

- Less time and less disposable income available for leisure than in later decades.
- Less leisure time spent at home as there were few TVs.
- Most people went on holiday in UK – only 2% of population travelled abroad.

Education

- Grammar schools – academic education, required the Eleven Plus exam to get in.
- Secondary modern schools – 70% of students went here in the 1950s.
- Secondary technical schools – very few in number.

Improving living and working conditions

Compared to life before the war, pay and working conditions were improving.

- ✓ Post-war economic boom: more jobs.
- ✓ Full employment.
- ✓ Welfare state: benefits for those in need.
- ✓ Wages increased faster than price.
- ✗ Unequal pay and opportunities for women.

The *Windrush* generation

Shortage of labour.

1948 British Nationality Act.

Recruitment drives.

Reasons for immigration

Support – e.g. loans.

Immigrant ambitions.

Positive view of Britain.

Riots and racism

Racism grew from concerns over:

- jobs
- mixed relationships
- benefits
- housing.

Notting Hill Race riots, 1958

Consequences of riots:

- anger about representations
- return of 4000 immigrants
- public opinion divided
- immigrant organisations set up
- government debates on immigration policies.

Now try this

Name **three** obstacles facing women in the 1950s who wanted the same opportunity to work and be promoted as men.

Education, work and labour relations c1960–79

Comprehensive education

- **Circular 10/65** – Crosland called for universal comprehensive education.
- 1966 – government put financial pressures on **LEAs** to go comprehensive.
- Supporters liked the equality of the system.
- Opponents felt comprehensives dragged down more able students and caused discipline problems.
- **1976 Education Act** (Labour) – education should not be based on selection.
- 1979 – Conservative government repealed Act but by then only 150 grammar schools left.

Educational opportunities

Students' educational opportunities were often affected more by choices made within schools than by the new comprehensive system.

Streaming within schools determined which students did O-Levels and which did no qualifications at all or the CSE exam, which was seen as a second-class qualification by employers. O-Levels were what employers wanted.

Government funding meant more students could go to university.

Reasons for changes in employment

Competition from other countries meant decline in traditional industries such as coal, shipbuilding and steel.

Higher disposable incomes increased demand for goods and services creating new jobs. Automation meant some manual jobs disappeared.

Changes in employment

Government spending created new public sector jobs.

Employment law – improving equality for women in work.

- Equal Pay Act (1970)
- Sex Discrimination Act (1975)
- Employment Protection Act (1975)

The three-day week

In February 1972, a 'three-day week' was declared where businesses were only allowed to use electricity on three consecutive days per week as a result of a dispute between the government and the NUM (National Union of Miners).

👎 Mining was in decline and uncompetitive.

👎 Miners demanded higher wages to keep up with inflation (rising prices).

👎 But the government needed lower wages to combat inflation.

👎 The miners went on strike, shutting down the supply of coal.

👎 Government declared a state of emergency and a three-day week.

👍 Government gave miners a pay increase in return for compromises.

| 6 October 1973 – Yom Kippur War. | → | 16 October 1973 – OPEC raise oil prices 70%. Global oil crisis. | → | High oil prices. February 1974 – miners' strike. 'Who governs Britain?' election. | → | New Labour government. Miners win 32% pay increase. | → | 1978 – 5% cap on pay increases triggered strikes. 1978–79 – 'Winter of Discontent'. By March pay rises 10–15% accepted. |

Now try this

Explain how inflation, wage demands and strikes are connected.

Media, communications and leisure c1960–79

Changes in media and entertainment

TV
- Far more leisure time spent at home.
- Spread new fashions.
- Programmes influenced public opinion.

Press
- News on TV led to decline in sales of newspapers.
- Newspapers became more sensationalist to increase sales.

Cinema
- Increase in TV watching led to huge drop in cinema visits.
- Many cinemas closed or changed function.
- Decline in British film making.

Changes

Records
- Dominated by Decca and EMI.
- Marketed new stars of rock and roll.
- EPs were better record format to LPs – jukeboxes could hold 500 EPs.

Radio
- Listener numbers not affected by TV – didn't compete.
- Transistor radios became fashionable – they were small and portable.
- 'Pirate' radio stations set up playing pop music – attracted millions of listeners.

The 'Swinging Sixties' – myth or reality?

Fashion: Mary Quant and Op Art, Biba, Carnaby Street, miniskirts.

Celebrity: models Jean Shrimpton and Twiggy; fashion photography.

Liberal attitudes: more permissive culture.

Music: 'Beatlemania', The Rolling Stones, 'The British Invasion' of US pop charts.

'Swinging London': global trendsetting capital – focus of 'Swinging Sixties' culture.

Image: British invention of 'cool' spread internationally by James Bond films and Mini cars.

Poverty – many were not able to buy new fashions.

The majority of people didn't change lifestyles.

Liberal attitudes were not found in most parts of UK.

Media attention focused on a small group of sixties icons.

The 'Swinging London' image was a tired cliché by 1967.

'Beatlemania' was created by record label promotion.

Changes in leisure

1 Youth culture – teenagers gain an identity.
- More teenagers due to baby boom.
- Better jobs meant more disposable income.

2 Entertainment became more home based.

3 Sport was a very popular pursuit.
- 1966 football World Cup in England.
- 1970s football affected by hooliganism.

4 Holidays – increase in package holidays to Mediterranean countries.

Now try this

Are the following Beatles facts true or false?

1 The Beatles were not actually able to play their instruments – they sang to a backing tape.

2 The Beatles pop tunes were written by Brian Epstein and George Martin.

3 Amazingly, no one was offended when John Lennon said The Beatles were 'more popular than Jesus'.

Reasons for social change c1960–79

Some reasons for changing social attitudes

Divorce made easier:
- 1969 Divorce Reform Act.
- 1970 Matrimonial Proceedings and Property Act.

Liberal Britain?

Contraception that women could control:
- 1961 contraceptive pill on sale.
- 1964 Brook clinics.
- 1967 Abortion legalised.
- 1974 contraceptive pill on prescription for all.

Homosexuality decriminalised:
- 1957 Wolfenden Report – but opposition.
- 1967 Sexual Offences Act.
- 1971 First gay march in London.
- Fear of homosexuality still very common in 1970s.

It is difficult to be sure how widespread liberal attitudes were in Britain, because people found it embarrassing to talk about their sex lives, affecting source reliability.

The abolition of the death penalty

In 1965, the death penalty was replaced by life imprisonment (with exceptions) and made permanent in 1969.

In favour of abolition:

Elite figures, e.g. influential MPs from all three main parties.

In favour of the death penalty:

Public opinion. Elite figures in House of Commons and Lords believed it was a deterrent.

Legislation for race relations

Race Relations Act 1968 – banned incitement to racial hatred and racial discrimination in public places.

- ✓ 1966: Race Relations Board set up to deal with complaints about racial discrimination.
- ✓ 1976 Race Relations Act – toughened laws against racial discrimination and set up Commission for Racial Equality.

However, Immigration Acts in 1968 and 1971 brought in some of the toughest anti-immigration laws in the world.

Equal pay for women

In 1968, Female sewing machinists went on strike to fight for equal pay with men doing a similar job in the Ford car plants at Dagenham and Halewood. The media and public opinion supported them, as did MP Barbara Castle. They won a pay deal of just over 90% of the men's earnings.

- ✓ The strike was a big influence in the passing of the 1970 Equal Pay Act.
- ✓ Equal opportunities improved throughout the 1970s.
- ✗ Women still under-represented in politics and in senior management positions.

Student protests

- Many students felt dissatisfied by the way the world was being run.
- War in Vietnam was a particular student flashpoint.

CND

- CND was founded in 1958.
- Large marches and demonstrations against nuclear weapons were arranged.

Feminism and Women's Lib

- Argued for equality for women with men in every aspect of life and work.
- There were influential organisations, personalities and publications.
- But most women in 1970s were not feminists and popular culture was sexist.

Now try this

1953: Derek Bentley; 1955: Ruth Ellis; 1950: Timothy Evans – choose one of these and explain why their death by hanging helped the case for the abolition of the death penalty from 1965.

Answers

International Relations: The Era of the Cold War 1943–1991

Key Topic 1: How did the Cold War in Europe develop? 1943–56

1 How did the Cold War begin?

1 Teheran Conference (1943): USA and UK to open second front in Europe to take pressure off USSR; USSR to declare war on Japan once Germany was defeated; Poland to receive land from defeated Germany, but have some taken away by USSR. Spheres of influence behind the discussions but not officially recorded: Eastern Europe for USSR, Western Europe for UK, USA and France.

Yalta Conference (1945): Germany to be reduced in size, divided, demilitarised; to be democratic and to pay reparations when defeated; Nazi Party to be banned and war criminals tried; United Nations would be set up to replace the League of Nations; the USSR would declare war on Japan after the defeat of Germany; the USSR would have land Japan had captured returned. Poland should be in the Soviet sphere of influence but democratic.

Potsdam Conference (1945): Set up a council of Foreign Ministers to organise the rebuilding of Europe. Nazi Party to be banned; surviving Nazis to be tried as war criminals in a special court run by the Allies at Nuremberg; reduce the size of Germany; divide Germany (and Berlin) into four zones, administered by the USA, the USSR, Britain and France, with the aim of reuniting it under one government as soon as possible; each country to take reparations from the zone they occupied, the USSR could have a quarter of the industrial equipment from the other three zones, because its zone was the least developed industrially, but had to provide the other zones with raw materials, such as coal.

2 That voters could only vote for communist candidates – other parties were not allowed.

2 Breakdown of trust

1 The table you have created will help you compare and contrast, often opposing terms / issues. It is fairly easy to create one for capitalism vs. communism as they are complete opposites of each other!

2 Communism's main criticism of capitalism was that it exploited the workers to make their bosses rich. Capitalism's criticism of communism was that it trampled on individual freedom and made everyone serve the state.

3 Satellite states, Cominform and Comecon

1 Cominform organised all the communist parties in Europe so they would do what the USSR told them. Comecon set up trade links between countries and prevented them joining the Marshall Plan.

2 Stalin thought that if countries got money from the Marshall Plan they would become dependent on the USA and reject the USSR.

4 The Truman Doctrine and the Marshall Plan

1 Reasons why President Truman was worried about communism spreading in Europe include: poverty and ruin in Europe made European people susceptible to communist propaganda; many European governments did not have the resources to fight against communist takeover; Eastern Europe had been liberated by Soviet troops, which gave the USSR a lot of influence in those countries.

2 The USA hoped that the Marshall Plan would combat the spread of communism by making people feel wealthier again and so giving them a stake in a capitalist future for their country.

5 The Berlin Blockade

1 **FRG** stands for Federal Republic of Germany (West Germany); **GDR** stands for German Democratic Republic (East Germany); **NATO** stands for North Atlantic Treaty Organization.

2 Because the USA had atomic weapons and the USSR did not.

6 Soviet control in Hungary

A timeline showing the key events in how the Cold War developed, 1943–56, would include such events as:

1943: Tehran Conference
1945: Yalta Conference and Potsdam Conference
1946: The Long Telegram and Novikov's Telegram
1947: Truman Doctrine announced
1947: Marshall Plan announced
1947: Cominform created
1948: Paris Conference
1948–49: Berlin Blockade
1949: Comecon created
1949: East Germany and West Germany created
1949: NATO formed
1955: Warsaw Pact formed
1956: Soviet invasion of Hungary

Key Topic 2: Three Cold War crises: Berlin, Cuba and Czechoslovakia c1957–69

7 A divided Berlin

1 The Warsaw Pact was the Soviet answer to NATO – a military alliance between the Eastern Bloc countries.

2 People in East Germany used West Berlin as a route into West Germany, especially skilled workers who could get better pay and conditions in the West. West Berlin also gave the USA a presence within Soviet-controlled Eastern Europe, from which it could spy on the USSR or try to influence events.

8 The Berlin Wall

1 The six-month ultimatum was the Soviet threat that the USA must remove its troops from Berlin within six months, or else…

2 **A** The Berlin Wall was built across Berlin.

9 The Cuban Missile Crisis: origins

The Bay of Pigs incident was an attempted overthrow of Fidel Castro's communist government of Cuba, led by Cubans who had left Cuba after the revolution and who opposed Castro. The attempted overthrow was secretly backed by the USA.

President Kennedy thought the Cubans would rise up to overthrow Castro – but, in fact, the opposite happened: the people fought to defend the revolution and the attempted overthrow was a failure. Kennedy thought Castro's control on Cuba was weak but because Castro knew about the invasion in advance, he was able to meet it with overwhelmingly superior troop numbers. Kennedy planned to replace Castro with Batista, the old leader of Cuba who was a strong supporter of the USA. However, most of the Cubans who hadn't left Cuba after the revolution were sick of Batista's corrupt leadership and did not want him back.

10 The Cuban Missile Crisis: the discovery

This answer depends on what advice you choose to give. Kennedy's advisors did think that an invasion might well be inevitable and all options appear to have been under serious consideration. The USA's superiority in nuclear weapons seriously weakened the USSR's position and you can see why the USSR's longer-term response to the crisis was to ensure the nuclear threat was more balanced between the two superpowers.

11 The Cuban Missile Crisis: the Thirteen Days

1 The USA had never been in range of USSR nuclear weapons before, while the USSR had been in range of US weapons since the end of the Second World War.

2 MAD stands for Mutually Assured Destruction. Because both sides knew that neither would survive a nuclear war, both sides worked to ensure a nuclear war did not happen: so to a big extent MAD did help keep the Cold War from turning into a hot war. But, because each side was very suspicious of the other, there were many points at which the USA or the USSR suspected the other side of planning to launch a strike, or developing new technology that would mean they could strike first and survive enough of the retaliation to then follow up with an invasion.

12 Soviet control in Czechoslovakia

A timeline showing the key events in the Cold War 1957–68 would include:
1957: Sputnik launched
1959: Geneva Summit
1960: Paris Conference
1961: Vienna Conference
1961: Bay of Pigs invasion
1962: Cuban Missile Crisis
1963: JFK visits Berlin
1963: Hotline set up between Washington D.C. and Moscow
1963: Limited Test Ban Treaty
1968: Prague Spring
1968: Soviet invasion of Czechoslovakia

Key Topic 3: Why did the Cold War end? From détente (1972) to the collapse of the Soviet Union (1991)

13 Détente

1 Détente means the relaxation of tension between rivals.

2 Nuclear non-proliferation meant working to stop the spread of nuclear weapons technology to other countries. The superpowers were interested in this, as they did not want the security threat of attacks from other countries to deal with. They did not want to be threatened with nuclear attacks by other countries and they did not want the balance of power between the two superpowers to be upset by other countries having nuclear weapons too.

14 The Soviet invasion of Afghanistan

1 Because of the USA's low-key reaction to Czechoslovakia in 1968, the USSR expected a similar reaction to the Soviet invasion of Afghanistan.

2 Reasons for the USA's strong reaction include: fear that détente had gone too far and weakened the USA against the USSR, and fear about Soviet influence in the oil-rich Middle East.

15 The Second Cold War, 1979–85

SDI changed the relationship between the USA and the USSR because SDI meant an end to MAD. If the USA could shoot down the USSR's intercontinental missiles then it had a major tactical advantage. (Not that the USA could do this!) The USSR's economy was not strong enough for it to develop a counter to SDI so the USSR was forced to undertake reforms to restructure its economy instead. In order to do this it also had to restructure its relationship with the west and Gorbachev had his biggest successes in this area of his reforms. UK Prime Minister Margaret Thatcher, a close ally of US President Ronald Reagan, famously said that the West could 'do business' with Gorbachev: a major shift in East–West international relations.

16 Gorbachev's new thinking

1 Gorbachev was keen to improve relations with the West because he needed a more open economy in the USSR and he needed to reduce the arms race in order to realign the USSR's economy away from building weapons.

2 Reagan was happy to reduce the number of nuclear weapons because he was confident that SDI would give the USA a major tactical advantage. The USA was also developing improved missile technology that would enable a smaller number of weapons to do the same amount of damage: basically he wasn't giving up any strategic advantage while it looked like the USSR probably was.

17 The break-up of the Eastern Bloc

Reasons why Gorbachev's reforms led to the end of the Warsaw Pact include: they allowed criticism of the Soviet Union, they allowed nationalism to develop into calls for independence and by ditching the Brezhnev Doctrine Gorbachev signalled that the Soviet Union would not crack down on any country that attempted to leave the Warsaw Pact.

18 The end of the Cold War

Three reasons to explain the end of the Cold War could include: the superiority of the capitalist model for generating growth; prosperity and technological developments; the exhaustion of the USSR caused by the arms race and the inefficiencies of the state planning of the economy; the war in Afghanistan; Gorbachev's misreading of the desire for independence among nationalities making up the USSR.

Unit 2A: Germany 1918–39

Key topic 1: The Weimar Republic 1918–29

20 The Weimar Republic 1918–23

The Treaty of Versailles included economic problems for the Republic, including reparations and loss of productive territory. The French occupation of the Ruhr also caused severe economic problems, particularly after German workers sabotaged production there. Bankruptcy and hyperinflation were economic problems.

21 Stresemann's successes at home and abroad

Stresemann was very important in the recovery: his actions stabilised the currency and restored confidence in the German economy and he recognised that Germany must restore international relationships if it was to recover its stability and get the loans it needed to rebuild. There are limitations to his achievements but the question doesn't ask about those.

Key topic 2: Hitler and the rise of the Nazi Party 1918–33

22 Hitler and the Nazi Party 1919–23

The French occupation of the Ruhr happened in 1923 after the German government announced that it could not pay reparations for 1923 and 1924. The French and Belgian governments decided that they should occupy the German industrial region of the Ruhr and run the industries there to make back what they were owed in reparations.

23 The years of struggle

1 Three factors could be: improvements to the German economy, a reduction in unemployment, a popular president of the Republic (Hindenburg).

2 Three ways of using propaganda could include: using new technology like radio and film; making sure the message was very clear and frequently repeated, using powerful images to make their intentions clear; making Hitler a figurehead for the Nazi Party – based around his charisma as a personal speaker. The Nazis also had close links with newspapers and newspaper owners: there were 120 Nazi newspapers in Germany (some of them daily and some weekly). Posters were also very important as a means of getting the Nazi message across and many of these were simple and striking to make the maximum impact.

24 The impact of the Great Depression

Reasons might include: unemployment – the Depression caused a huge rise in unemployment and the Weimar government's failure to solve this problem contrasted with the Nazis' apparent solutions. Weimar tax increases were made necessary by the lack of money available to the government (given its determined attempt to avoid hyperinflation again), but they made the government extremely unpopular at a time when so many families were plunged into poverty. Again, the Nazis were able to benefit from this unpopularity and from their promises to rebuild Germany without reliance on foreign loans. The weakness of the Weimar coalition governments meant that finding a way out of the Depression was even harder than it might otherwise have been, which again contrasted strongly with the Nazis' strong leadership and clear messages.

25 Who supported the Nazis 1929–33?

1 Farmers had not benefited from the recovery under Stresemann and feared the communists a lot because the communists would take their land away from them if they got into power. So they were receptive to the Nazis anyway and then the Nazis made sure they promised the farmers a key role in rebuilding Germany.

2 The Nazis did have some success with getting votes from the workers, the biggest electoral group, but the communists had a better offer for the poorest workers – that they would create a workers' state like the Bolsheviks had done in Russia. The Nazis had more appeal to the middle classes because they were terrified of communists taking all their possessions away from them.

26 Hitler becomes chancellor

1 Following the July 1932 elections, the Nazis were the largest party in the Reichstag but didn't have a majority. Hitler demanded to be made chancellor but Hindenburg didn't like the fact that Hitler was a 'nobody' and didn't trust him. Instead, he made von Papen

chancellor. Von Papen had no support in the Reichstag and had to call another election, which also made the Nazis the largest single party in November 1932. This time Hindenburg, after rejecting Hitler again, chose von Schleicher. But von Schleicher also had no support and had to resign after a month. Hitler was then offered the post of chancellor, because he did have the support needed to get laws passed in the Reichstag. Hitler became chancellor in January 1933.

2 The mistake Hindenburg and von Papen made was to assume that because there were only a few Nazis in the cabinet and lots of their own people, they would be able to control what the government did: they would tell Hitler what laws needed to be passed, he'd go and get the votes needed in the Reichstag and their problems would be solved. The Nazis had lost 38 seats in the November 1932 election so it looked like the Hitler bubble had burst. Once he became chancellor, however, Hitler used the resources at his command to set up the Nazi takeover of Germany.

Key topic 3: The Nazi dictatorship 1933–39

27 Removing the opposition

1 The Nazis used fear of communism, oppression of communist opponents and state-backed propaganda to win the March 1933 election with 288 seats. Backed by another small party they had a majority in the Reichstag. Hitler used the SA and the SS to threaten and intimidate the Reichstag into passing the Enabling Act, with only the SPD (120 seats) daring to oppose it.

2 The Enabling Act was so significant because it meant Hitler could do pretty much anything he wanted – he didn't need Hindenburg's agreement to pass a new law, he could just go ahead and pass it.

28 The Nazi police state

1 The Gestapo was the secret police force of the Nazi regime. They had the power to arrest anyone and send anyone to a concentration camp without needing to use the courts or giving any justification at all. This was obviously a very easy way to get rid of any opposition, actual or suspected. Fear of the Gestapo was a very powerful feature of Nazi control, as well as what they actually did.

2 The law courts were completely controlled by the Nazis and this meant that anyone who did go to court accused of actions against the Nazi regime would not get a fair trial.

29 Controlling and influencing attitudes

1 Nazi propaganda like this reinforced Hitler's image as a wonderfully wise, determined leader, completely committed to making Germany great again. Everything in the picture is designed to show leadership: his strong pose, his clenched fist, and his firm gaze to the horizon and Germany's great future. The caption is strong and simple and puts Hitler, as Führer, right at the heart of what many Germans wanted: a greater Germany, without the non-Germans who had been dragging it down, all working together as a nation under the strong leadership of an inspired Führer.

2 Cheap mass-produced radios meant that the maximum number of people could afford to buy them, which meant Nazi radio propaganda would reach its biggest possible market. Hitler's speeches were very effective means of propaganda and the radio was the best way of ensuring that these speeches were heard by as many Germans as possible.

Key topic 4: Nazi domestic policies 1933–39

30 Nazi policies towards the young and women

(a) Three points showing Nazis' policies towards young people and women were a success could include: strong support for the Nazis amongst most young people; Nazi control of what children were taught at school and during leisure time must have had an impact; there was a decline in the number of married women in employment 1933–36, in line with Nazi policy, the number of marriages increased, in line with Nazi policy, and there was an increase in the number of babies born, which the Nazis also promoted.

(b) Three points suggesting the policies did not work all that well could include: the Edelweiss Pirates showed that not all children were indoctrinated. Nazi policy on women workers had to be adjusted in the late 1930s because of a shortage of workers, the rise in marriages would probably have happened anyway as economic conditions got better and most women continued to have two children, not the four children minimum the Nazis were hoping for.

31 Employment and the standard of living

The Nazis certainly did focus a lot of effort on reducing the numbers of unemployed. The Nazi policy of rearmament created a lot of new jobs both directly through the arms industry (spending on rearmament increased from 3.5 billion marks in 1933 to 26 billion marks in 1939) and because rearmament required a lot more iron and steel: they were both big industries that employed a lot of people. There were many other reasons too, some of them linked to rearmament, such as conscription, which saw large numbers of young men taken out of unemployment for military service, and some of them independent of rearmament, such as the RAD and the encouragement for women to stay at home rather than work. Hitler came to power as the Depression was ending and economic recovery may have been happening regardless of specific policies such as rearmament. So while rearmament was certainly an important part of the fall in unemployment through the boost it gave to industry, it was only one reason amongst many.

32 Nazi persecution

The changes in Nazi persecution of the Jews from 1933 to 1939 are a series of steps towards a goal: the removal of Jews from greater Germany. In 1933 Jews were banned from government jobs and the army, from public places in 1934 and in 1935 the Nuremburg Laws stripped Jews of all rights of German citizenship and made them completely separate. From 1938 the Nazis geared up for a physical removal of Jews, with laws that Jews had to register all their possessions and carry identity cards. *Kristallnacht* in November 1938 saw state-sponsored attacks on Jews, followed by thousands of Jews being sent to concentration camps. In April 1939 all Jews were to be evicted from their homes and sent to ghettos and other easily controlled areas.

Unit 2B: Russia 1914–39

Key topic 1: The Tsarist regime and its collapse 1914–17

33 Social inequality in Russia, 1914

This answer depends on your own point of view: many historians would give a high priority to the impact of rapid urbanisation, Russia's disastrous First World War and Nicholas II's character, but you could make a case for many others too.

34 The impact of the First World War

1 Answers to include: it was poorly equipped, badly trained, difficult for soldiers to reach the Front due to poor transport system.

2 Because the Tsar, against the advice of his own cabinet, took personal command of the army, after which all problems in the war were blamed directly on him. Leaving his wife in charge of the country meant her mistakes were blamed on him, too.

35 The fall of the Tsar

1 If you interpreted Marx like Lenin did then the February Revolution was inevitable, but to most historians it was spontaneous – it wasn't planned and in fact took the Bolsheviks off guard.

2 Soviet means council in Russian and workers and soldiers formed their own soviets to represent their interests.

Key topic 2: Bolshevik takeover and consolidation 1917–24

36 Provisional Government problems

Peace meant an end to the First World War; land meant distribution of land to those who work it, and bread meant an end to food shortages and bread rationing. These were all powerful and simple messages that resonated with soldiers and the families of soldiers, with the peasants (to a certain extent), and with urban Russians who were desperate for more food.

37 The October Revolution

There is no doubt that the Provisional Government was very unpopular by the time of the October 1917 Revolution. The events of the February 1917 Revolution and July Days showed that popular discontent with food shortages, rationing, unemployment, as well as the state of the economy in towns and cities (and peasant discontent about land ownership in the country) could and did result in revolutionary activity. But the October Revolution was different in several ways from earlier uprisings against the failures of the Provisional Government. The Bolsheviks carefully planned their seizure of power, making sure they had control of the Petrograd Soviet, organising control of key Petrograd locations and, most significantly perhaps, achieving the takeover with a relatively small number of supporters. The Bolsheviks organised the October Revolution in order to seize power before the Provisional Government could organise elections for a new national government that represented all parts of society. So it could be argued that the Bolsheviks took control while the Provisional Government was still unpopular, rather than because of this unpopularity.

38 Bolsheviks in control?

1 The Social Revolutionaries did so well because they represented the peasants (the vast majority of the electorate) and had always represented the peasants. The peasants trusted them more than they trusted the Bolsheviks.

2 The Bolsheviks needed the war to be over so they could concentrate on establishing control over Russia and on fighting off the inevitable counter-revolution, but the Bolshevik leadership was also convinced that there was going to be a revolution in Germany at any moment, so it didn't really matter what the terms were. In fact, the initial terms demanded by Germany were not as harsh but the Bolsheviks delayed, waiting for the revolution that never came, during which time the German forces advanced almost to Petrograd. And that was another reason – German troops reaching the capital.

39 The civil war

1 The Cheka were the Bolsheviks' secret police. They helped the Bolsheviks keep power by crushing any political opposition. During the civil war the Cheka was the leading force in the Red Terror, which arrested 87 000 people and shot 8389 of them. Not only did this remove actual political opponents of the Bolsheviks, it also removed people who were suspected of opposition and scared almost everyone else into doing what the Bolsheviks said.

2 War Communism was a system of state control that made sure the Red Army got the food and equipment it needed at the expense of everyone else. War Communism certainly helped the Bolsheviks win the civil war, which kept them in power, but it also set up a harsh control of people's lives that tried to make everyone serve the needs of the state, rather than do what they wanted for themselves.

40 Creating a new society

War Communism was a very strict form of communism in which state control took from everyone and gave back the most to those who were doing the most for the state: the Red Army in particular. There was no market for food – the state took food from the peasants and left them just a small amount to live on. The state took complete control of industry and organised it to make what the state needed to win the war. Strikes were banned. The state also used the Cheka to eliminate any opposition and to try and make all the people committed to serving the state above their own interests.

The impact of all this was that the Bolsheviks won the civil war, but at a high cost, including the Kronstadt Mutiny. The NEP was a reluctant step back from communism: it reintroduced a market for food and stopped taking food from the peasants, it returned small factories to private ownership and allowed the manufacture of things for profit. Money came back in, and anyone could start a shop and sell products for profit.

Key topic 3: The nature of Stalin's dictatorship 1924–39

41 Stalin's struggle for power

As General Secretary, Stalin was in charge of who got the different jobs within the Communist Party and he made sure he appointed people to the top jobs who would support him. Using this power base, he would then start rumours against rivals and isolate them and any supporters they had from the party, until the party agreed to expel them or put them on trial.

42 Terror in the 1930s

The purges had a wide range of effects: they killed around a million people and put 7 million people in prison/forced labour camps. This meant that most of the survivors knew someone who was purged and that created an atmosphere of fear and suspicion amongst all the population – since few of the people arrested had ever appeared to be traitors before. As well as fear of being surrounded by hidden traitors, some people also distrusted the secret police (although few people thought that Stalin was to blame) and the justice system. The loss of so many people meant skills were lost at all levels, especially in the army and the Communist Party, from industry and from agriculture. No one dared to criticise Stalin and this meant any mistakes he made were never challenged.

43 Censorship and propaganda

Making Lenin into a cult figure meant that the October Revolution and the civil war took on a sort of holy character that were beyond criticism. Lenin had interpreted the words of Marx and brought all the wonders of socialism to Russia. Stalin portrayed himself as Lenin's successor (even though Lenin hadn't been very positive about him) and that put him beyond criticism too.

Key topic 4: Economic and social changes 1928–39

44 Collectivisation

Three reasons could include: a need to increase food production; a need to make agriculture more socialist; a need to get control over the peasant population.

45 Industrialisation

Key features of industrialisation under Stalin would include: all based on Five-Year Plans, which set out what was going to be produced and also set targets for how much should be produced; industry was also predominantly heavy industry, often in factories built from scratch in places where the state decided they needed to be. Industrialisation was also extremely rapid, involved slave labour to a certain extent via the gulag prison camp system, and depended also on propaganda-led Stakhanovite efforts. Women were a key part of the workforce, with state provision of childcare to allow this.

46 Life in the Soviet Union

The poster includes some interesting details that back up its message of life becoming better for Soviet citizens each day: the woman wears a wristwatch and is standing by a car. She has a medal on her chest, suggesting she has earned these good things by serving the state. She is standing and looking into the future in a field of wheat – representing there being plenty of food for everyone. Electricity pylons represent development of all rural areas of Russia and also industrialisation – this is a modern country. The background shows a busy river with boats taking raw materials to industry but also people having fun on the river.

This might have been an accurate picture for a very small number of party members but for most Soviet citizens life was not very often like this. Very few citizens had cars and if they had wristwatches, then, they were cheap, badly made and frequently in need of repair. Basic food might have been available but there were not many consumer goods to buy and most urban families relied on relatives in the countryside or their own garden plots for fresh vegetables. Many urban families lived in a single room, often sharing a kitchen and toilet with many other families. And many families may not have viewed the future with such optimism: there was a Soviet joke about work: 'We pretend to work and they pretend to pay us'.

Unit 2C: The USA 1919–41

Key topic 1: The US economy 1919–41

47 The USA after the First World War

1 The Tariff Acts led to a decline because other countries put up tariffs of their own on US goods, which meant fewer exports were sold.

2 It would argue that wages were none of its business.

48 Problem areas

US farming, especially in the southern states, was heavily dependent on cotton growing so the development of artificial fabrics that replaced cotton was not good news for US farming.

49 The US economic boom

1 Causes of the economic boom could include: huge demand for US products in war-torn Europe; opening up of new markets following break up of European empires; lots of innovation in the USA; high confidence in US economy and society; mass production techniques and the development of new ways of advertising products.

2 Mass production reduces prices because the producer can make more products for less money and in less time, so more can be sold at a cheaper price and still make the producer more money as a result.

Key topic 2: US society 1919–29

50 The roaring 20s

1   After the First World War, women were given equal voting rights to men because the government recognised the role they had played in helping to win the war. This was a significant change. Women had had jobs in the war but were expected to give them up again when men came back from the war, so for many women life in the 1920s was less different from before the war than during it. But for 'flappers' – young women who wore modern clothes, smoked and drank, had jobs and had fun – the 1920s were a very different experience. Although most flappers married and settled back to a life like their mothers', attitudes to women changed significantly as a result of what the flappers did and stood for.

2   Advertising and consumerism targeted women as a market. Products aimed at reducing household chores like cleaning, washing, storing food and cooking meals meant that women did not have to work so hard or for so long on housework and had a bit more leisure time. Fashion and lifestyle products were aimed at women who had a bit more free time and a bit more money to spend. These products could spread new ideas about what US women were doing with their lives and these ideas could influence women around the USA in different ways.

51 Prohibition and gangsters

Soldiers had been trained to use guns and had seen a lot of violence, death and destruction. When they came back to the USA, some men looked for the excitement of war again, while some felt unable to reconnect with their old lives and ambitions.

52 Racism and intolerance

The Scopes 'Monkey Trial' was about intolerance: some religious groups did not believe children should be taught the theory of evolution and this was state law in some parts of the USA, even though the US Constitution granted everyone the right to believe what they wanted.

Key topic 3: The USA in Depression 1929–33

53 The Wall Street Crash

Your own definitions of these key terms might be worded differently from these ones – that's good as you are more likely to remember your own definitions. **Bankruptcy** is when a person or company is officially unable to pay their debts: when this happens all their property is transferred to a trustee who then uses it to pay back creditors. An **investor** is someone who puts money into an enterprise, usually by buying shares in that enterprise, in the hope of making more money when the enterprise is successful and the value of their shares goes up. **Shares** are a share in a company that people can buy: sometimes people buy shares to get a regular dividend payment from the company, sometimes they buy them hoping that the company will go up in value so they will be able to sell the shares for more than they paid for them. **Credit** is a type of debt: people can buy things on credit which means they don't pay for them immediately but later. **Loans** are when someone gives money to someone else, and that person agrees to pay it back.

54 Hoover's reaction

One example would be the tax cut of 1930: taxes are how the government gets money to spend so a tax cut is basically a government saying we won't do as much for you, you need to do it for yourself. The argument is that if people know they will keep more of their money for themselves rather than pay it out in tax they will work harder, create more jobs and make more money and help the country that way.

55 The impact of the Depression

Reasons for the election defeat could include: perception that he was helping the rich and not the poor, that he was not doing enough to create jobs for the unemployed, and that he expected too much from volunteer charities who actually needed more support from the government to deal with the scale of the Depression.

Key topic 4: Roosevelt and the New Deal 1933–41

56 The New Deal

AAA = Agricultural Adjustment Act
NRA = National Recovery Administration
FERA = Federal Emergency Relief Administration
CCC = Civilian Conservation Corps

57 Opposition and the Second New Deal

1   The main criticism was that the Alphabet Agencies went against the US constitution by letting federal government interfere in things that were covered by the laws of individual states.

2   Father Coughlin was a Catholic priest with an audience of over 30 million listeners to his weekly radio talks. His National Union of Social Justice criticised FDR's government and Father Coughlin supported Huey Long's bid to run for president.

In 1934, the Schechter Poultry Co. was prosecuted for breaking NRA (National Recovery Administration) codes. This became known as the 'sick chicken case'. The company appealed to the Supreme Court on the grounds that the NRA couldn't prosecute them on a federal matter when they only sold their chickens in one state. The Supreme Court found in their favour, which was the beginning of a run of decisions by the Supreme Court that declared New Deal Agencies illegal.

58 Was the New Deal a success?

The Second World War helped the USA recover from the Depression because the war created big new markets for arms, ammunition and food amongst the USA's allies, which was set up on a loan basis using Roosevelt's Lend-Lease scheme. Then when the USA entered the war itself, it rearmed for that too.

Unit 3A: War and the transformation of British society c1903–28

60 Britain c1903–28 What skills do I need?

Your definitions should be similar to these ones:

*   Inferences – working something out from what the source says / shows.
*   Purpose of a source – purpose is what the source was written or created for, the effect it is trying to achieve.
*   Reliability – how far you can trust a source, whether you believe what it says or shows.
*   Causation – explaining why something happened.
*   Hypothesis – a particular view of the event or person that the question is about.
*   Evaluating – judging the value of something.

61 Five question types

(a)   Inference.
(b)   Evaluating a hypothesis.

62 Skills in practice

1   The content of a source means the information a source gives you about a person or an event.

2 The context of a source is related to the knowledge you already have about a topic that the source is connected to.

63 Nature, origin and purpose
Content: The photo shows two women making explosives.
Context: During the Great War, many women took on roles traditionally reserved for men in order to help the war effort.
Origins: The photo is posed suggesting that it might have been taken by an official government photographer.
Purpose: The purpose may have been to show that women were capable of doing useful war work and to encourage others to do the same. This may have been part of a government propaganda campaign.
Nature: This is a formal posed photograph.

64 Applying your skills
The answer to question 1 is fine, as it gives an inference and supports it with a 'because the source says…' statement. However, it could be improved with a second inference, for example, that artillery methods had not yet been developed that could effectively counter this new weapon.

The answer to the question 4 needs some improvement. The answer is OK in saying what is useful about the source, but there needs to be more on nature and origin – who was it written by and why is that significant, and its usefulness needs to be compared with the student's own knowledge in order to get top marks. Reliability should also be considered.

65 The Liberals and social reform
(a) The Children's Charter gave children legal protection from neglect, banned them from buying fireworks, tobacco or alcohol and set up juvenile courts and borstals so they were no longer sent to adult prisons. The School Meals Act meant they could get fed at school for free, and medical inspections were introduced to improve health.
(b) The Old Age Pensions Act meant that the very poorest people over 70 received a small pension.
(c) Labour exchanges helped workers find jobs. The National Insurance Act gave workers some limited health insurance, and provided support for some workers if they were unemployed.

66 The part played by the British on the Western Front
The combination of trenches, barbed wire and machine guns meant that it was much easier to defend the front line than it was to attack and break through the enemy's lines. Well-established trenches had deep bunkers where troops could shelter from artillery bombardments. When the artillery bombardment stopped, the troops could rush out and man the machine guns that could fire on every inch of no-man's land. As the enemy infantry slowly advanced, cutting their way through barbed wire defences, the machine guns could cut them all down. Even if the enemy succeeded in taking the front line trenches, there were lines and lines of trenches behind the front line from where a counter-attack could be launched.

67 The Home Front and social change 1914–18
Your three reasons could include:
- Government propaganda meant most people strongly believed that men should sign up to defend the country.
- At a time when the whole country was focused on defeating the Germans, people felt that conscientious objectors (COs) were helping the enemy. Time and money had to be spent on tribunals, on feeding and guarding those COs who were imprisoned, etc.
- Usually at least one member of a CO tribunal was military or ex-military. This meant that very few COs were treated fairly. Few were judged to be refusing to serve due to firmly held moral beliefs.

- People who had lost family and friends already in the war felt the sacrifices their loved ones had made were cheapened by conscientious objectors acting like they had a choice. The strongest critics of COs were often women, who were usually facing the fact that their husbands, boyfriends, brothers, sons were away fighting and might not come back.

68 Economic and social change 1918–28
The government portrayed the General Strike as a threat of revolution and an attack on democracy. In a democracy, people use their vote to get the change they want, rather than taking action into their own hands. The TUC certainly did not see the General Strike as a revolution: it was an industrial dispute and the TUC worked hard to keep it peaceful. A balanced view would accept that there were some strikers who wanted a revolution and the TUC was not able to control these strikers, so there was violence. However, the portrayal of the strike by the government was not a fair representation of what the majority of strikers wanted to achieve – the fair treatment for working people within the existing political system.

Unit 3B: War and the transformation of British society c1931–51

69 Britain c1931–51 What skills do I need?
Your definitions should be similar to these ones:
- Inferences – working something out from what the source says / shows.
- Purpose of a source – purpose is what the source was written or created for, the effect it is trying to achieve.
- Reliability – how far you can trust a source, whether you believe what it says or shows.
- Causation – explaining why something happened.
- Hypothesis – a particular view of the event or person that the question is about.
- Evaluating – judging the value of something.

70 Five question types
(a) Inference.
(b) Evaluating a hypothesis.

71 Skills in practice
1 The content of a source means the information a source gives you about a person or an event.
2 The context of a source is related to the knowledge you already have about a topic that the source is connected to.

72 Nature, origin and purpose
Content: The painting shows scenes of Britain's leaders and ordinary people pulling together to cope with the Blitz.
Context: During the Blitz, London was bombed intensively by the Germans with the aim of damaging British morale as well as houses and factories.
Origins: Painted in 1942, just after the Blitz and while the war was still raging.
Purpose: Probably created to remind British people how they had all pulled together to survive the Blitz. The aim was to improve morale and stiffen people's resolve to continue the war.
Nature: A propaganda painting.

73 Applying your skills
The answer to question 1 is fine as it gives an inference and supports it with a 'because the source says…' statement. It needs another inference and supporting statement to maximise marks, however.

The answer to the question 4 needs some improvement. The answer is OK as it considers nature and origin, but its usefulness needs to be compared with the student's own knowledge in order to get top marks. The content needs to be considered.

In the exam there will also be a second source for this question type (not included here), and so a full answer would evaluate reliability for both.

74 The impact of the Depression 1931–39

Many of the officials and members of the NUWM were communists and the people of Jarrow did not want their march, which was for jobs, to be seen as a political protest, especially not a communist protest as this would turn a lot of public opinion against the marchers.

75 Britain at war 1939–45

Your three reasons could include:

- The USA – its vast industrial capacity meant that the Allies had far more weaponry than the Germans and while the Germans were running out of reinforcements, the Allies could easily replace troops with new recruits.
- Hitler's decision to invade the Soviet Union was a major strategic error which meant that Germany had to fight the Allies on two fronts: one in the west and south and one to the east against the Soviet Union.
- The failure of the *Luftwaffe* to beat the Allies in the air meant the Allies could support their troops from the air and, critically, could bomb German industry and cities far more heavily than Britain was bombed in the Blitz.
- D-Day was well planned.

76 The Home Front 1939–45

Your three points could include:

- Women took over what had traditionally been 'men's work' in agriculture, manufacturing (including munitions work) and service industries (jobs like bus and train conductors had usually been for men before the war).
- From December 1941, unmarried women between the ages of 20 and 30 were conscripted, choosing between work in the armed services (not fighting roles though) and key industries.
- For mothers in urban centres, evacuation from September 1939 separated many from their young children, which was a very difficult experience for many.
- Women usually did the shopping and cooking in this period and rationing meant that what they could buy and what they could cook was significantly restricted.

77 Labour in power 1945–51

Your answers might include:

- People felt that all the sacrifices of the war should amount to something better for everyone in the future – not just a return to how things had been.
- The state had shown during the war that it was capable of organising things so that everyone got enough. Many people felt that before the war, it was the rich that got the best of everything while everyone else had to make do with what was left.
- The 1930s had been a miserable time of economic depression for many British people, and many thought the state had not done enough to help people survive the Depression.

Unit 3C: The transformation of British society c1951–79

78 Britain c1951–79 What skills do I need?

Your definitions should be similar to these ones:

- Inferences – working something out from what the source says / shows.
- Purpose of a source – purpose is what the source was written or created for, the effect it is trying to achieve.
- Reliability – how far you can trust a source, whether you believe what it says or shows.
- Causation – explaining why something happened.
- Hypothesis – a particular view of the event or person that the question is about.
- Evaluating – judging the value of something.

79 Five question types

(a) Inference.

(b) Evaluating a hypothesis.

80 Skills in practice

1 The content of a source means the information a source gives you about a person or an event.

2 The context of a source is related to the knowledge you already have about a topic that the source is connected to.

81 Nature, origin and purpose

Content: The source shows a man about to throw a binbag onto a huge pile of rubbish on one side of a road. The man has another bag of rubbish on top of his car which he is presumably going to add to the pile.

Context: In the Winter of Discontent (1979), there were many public service strikes, including refuse collection. As a result, uncollected rubbish from houses, businesses and public works like hospitals, built up in the streets.

Origins: Unclear who took the photo.

Purpose: Unclear who took the photo or why, but the shot is framed so as to show the large number of people present. It may have been taken to demonstrate the strength of the anti-Vietnam protest movement.

Nature: This is a contemporary photo taken during the Winter of Discontent.

82 Applying your skills

1 The answer to question 1 is fine as it gives an inference and supports it with a 'because the source says…' statement. It needs another inference and supporting statement to maximise marks.

2 The answer to question 2 needs some improvement. The answer uses the source and own knowledge to explain one factor of the question (though a quotation from the source to back up this explanation would have made this explanation more secure). Now the answer needs to explain a second factor: for example, it could use own knowledge to explain that the songwriting skills of Lennon and McCartney were also highly significant in ensuring The Beatles' success: perhaps an area that George Harrison felt excluded from, making his account unrepresentative of all members of The Beatles.

83 British society and economy in the 1950s

Your three obstacles could include:

- There were no laws enforcing quality of pay or equality of opportunity.
- Girls were not typically encouraged at school to think about further education or training for a career in a specialist job.
- Few women went to university, and those that did rarely studied for professions like medicine, law or engineering.
- Employers did not like giving jobs to women who had young children as they thought they would often need to take time off work to care for them.
- The view that most people shared was that it was right for a women to get married, have children and stay at home to care for them. Anyone who chose differently would stand out.
- Most jobs were in traditionally male areas: industry and manufacturing.

84 Education, work and labour-relations 1960–79

Inflation can happen when rising costs means people need to be paid more, which means producers put up costs further: pushing inflation higher and higher. When prices are rising then there are demands by workers to be paid more, because otherwise a lot more of their wage has to be spent on things like food and fuel than before, making them feel poorer. But governments try to reduce inflation by putting caps on wages to slow down the 'inflationary spiral'. This is unpopular with workers, who may then be more likely to vote for strike action. If the workers are producing something that a lot of people need, a strike can put a lot of pressure on the government.

85 Media, communications and leisure c1960–79

1 Absolutely false!
2 False: their most famous songs were almost all written by John Lennon and Paul McCartney.
3 False: many British people were very upset by the remarks which were seen as blasphemous.

86 Reasons for social change c1960–79

Derek Bentley was hanged in 1953 but there was public concern about the fact he was only 19, had learning difficulties and that the evidence against him was not clear-cut. Ruth Ellis was hanged in 1955 and public opinion was against her being killed because she had three young children and had been abused by her lover, whom she killed. Timothy Evans was hanged in 1950 for killing his baby daughter, but then evidence was found suggesting a serial killer had been responsible. A posthumous pardon was issued in 1966 (the first ever such pardon) which convinced many people that the death penalty should be abolished because innocent people could be wrongly convicted and wrongly deprived of life.

This page has been intentionally left blank.

This page has been intentionally left blank.

This page has been intentionally left blank.

This page has been intentionally left blank.

This page has been intentionally left blank.

This page has been intentionally left blank.

Published by Pearson Education Limited, 80 Strand, London, WC2R 0RL.

www.pearsonschoolsandfecolleges.co.uk

Copies of official specifications for all Pearson qualifications may be found on the website: www.edexcel.com

Text © Pearson Education Limited 2015
Edited by Lucy Tritton, Alison Cornwell and Wearset Ltd, Boldon, Tyne and Wear
Typeset by Tech-Set Ltd, Gateshead and Tek-Art, West Sussex
Original illustrations © Pearson Education Limited 2015
Illustrated by KJA Artists
Cover illustration by Miriam Sturdee

The right of Rob Bircher to be identified as author of this work has been asserted by him in accordance with the
Copyright, Designs and Patents Act 1988.

First published 2015

18 17 16
10 9 8 7 6 5 4 3 2

British Library Cataloguing in Publication Data
A catalogue record for this book is available from the British Library

ISBN 978 1 292 09712 1

Acknowledgements

The author and publisher would like to thank the following individuals and organisations for permission to reproduce
photographs:

(Key: b-bottom; c-centre; l-left; r-right; t-top)

akg-images Ltd: 12, ullstein bild 9; **Alamy Images:** Brian Harris 76, INTERFOTO 10b, MARKA 1, The Art
Archive 40t; **Corbis:** Bettmann 50, Hulton-Deutsch Collection 36, Peter Turnley 16, 17tr, Sygma / JP Laffont 17tl,
Sygma / Thomas Johnson 42; **Daily Express:** Michael Cummings cartoon 09 / 02 / 1973 79; **FotoLibra:** World
History Archive 74; **Getty Images:** AFP 6, 40b, Hulton Archive 10t, 21; **Library of Congress:** 15l; **London School
of Economics and Political Science:** From LSE Library Collections 58; **Mary Evans Picture Library:** Jazz Age
Club Collection 49, Malcolm Greensmith Collection 67, The March of the Women Collection 61, Weimar Archive 4;
Photoshot Holdings Limited: 28b, World Illustrated 32; **Rex Features:** 28t; **The Art Archive:** Culver Pictures 73;
TopFoto: 72, Granger Collection 34, HIP / The LordPrice Collection 70

All other images © Pearson Education Limited

We are grateful to the following for permission to reproduce copyright material:
Extract on page 64 from *The Old Front Line* by John Masefield, 1917 published by Pen & Sword Ltd/William
Heinemann, p.31; extract on page 73 from an interview from Mass Observation in 1944. www.massobs.org.uk.
Reproduced with permission of Curtis Brown Group Ltd, London on behalf of the Trustees of the Mass Observation
Archive, copyright © The Trustees of the Mass Observation Archive; extract on page 82 from "At the Crossroads",
Daily Mirror, 11/11/1966, p.9 (Don Short), copyright © Mirrorpix 1966.

Every effort has been made to contact copyright holders of material reproduced in this book. Any omissions will be
rectified in subsequent printings if notice is given to the publishers.